Houghton Mifflin Reading

Rewards

Senior Authors
J. David Cooper
John J. Pikulski

Authors
Kathryn Au
David J. Chard
Gilbert Garcia
Claude Goldenberg
Phyllis Hunter
Marjorie Y. Lipson
Shane Templeton
Sheila Valencia
MaryEllen Vogt

Consultants
Linda H. Butler
Linnea C. Ehri
Carla Ford

HOUGHTON MIFFLIN

BOSTON

Cover illustration copyright © 2005 by Gerald McDermott.

Acknowledgments begin on page 447.

Printed in the U.S.A.

ISBN: 0-618-24147-7

3 4 5 6 7 8 9 DW 09 08 07 06 05 04

Rewards

Theme 1

Off to Adventure!

Theme Wrap-Up

Check Your Progress

POETRY

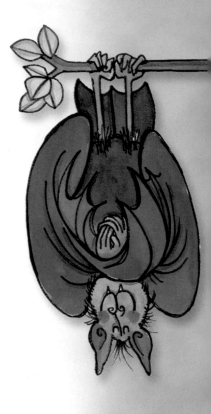

Theme 2

Celebrating Traditions

5

Celebrating Traditions

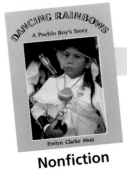
Theme Wrap-Up
Check Your Progress

Focus on Genre
TRICKSTER TALES

Theme 3

Incredible Stories

Theme Wrap-Up
Check Your Progress

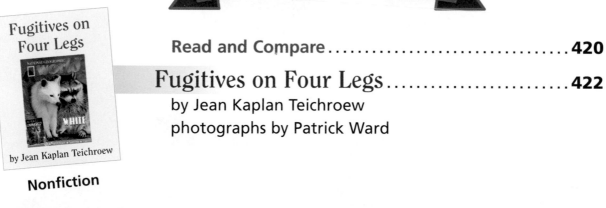

10

Theme 1

Off to Adventure!

Can't keep still all day. . . .

I like adventures, and

I'm going to find one.

from Little Women
by Louisa May Alcott

Off to Adventure!

with Mark Teague

Get ready to set off on a reading adventure! Read this letter from theme author Mark Teague.

Dear Adventurers,

   I will keep this brief, because I know that you are ready to get going on your adventure. Before you begin, there are a few items you should have with you.

   First, you will need a good pair of walking shoes. Adventurers do a lot of walking. You will also need climbing shoes, and riding boots wouldn't be a bad idea either. Also, you should bring along swim fins, roller skates, and galoshes, just in case.

   Don't forget insect repellent. Adventures can get very buggy. For that matter, thunderstorm repellent, hurricane repellent, and invading army repellent could all come in handy. While you're at it, bring along a suit of armor.

I also suggest that you take a pogo stick for jumping, an inflatable raft with paddles, a space helmet, and a very small airplane.

Finally, don't forget a change of clothes and a toothbrush. This will make your mother happy.

See? That didn't take long. Now you're ready for your very own adventure. Send me a postcard. Oh, and bring this book. You'll want something good to read!

Sincerely,

Mark Teague

ADVENTURE

14

Have an Adventure

Think about what Mark Teague says you should bring on your own adventure. How might some of these items help you?

Look at the book covers below to see what adventures you are going to have. As you read each selection, ask yourself how the characters are alike and different.

Get ready to climb a cliff, ride a horse, and rescue a family from danger. It's time to get started!

Internet

To learn about the authors in this theme, visit Education Place. **www.eduplace.com/kids**

Cliff Hanger

JEAN CRAIGHEAD GEORGE
WENDELL MINOR

Read to find the meanings of these words.

e • Glossary

belay
descent
harness
ledge
rappel
trekked

Rock Climbing

Have you ever **trekked** up a mountain? What was the **descent** like? Was it scary coming down from the mountain?

One way people get to the top of some mountains is to rock climb. Learning how to rock climb takes a lot of strength and practice. There are many ways climbers make sure they are safe.

A **harness** is a set of straps attached to a rope. The harness supports the climber as he or she climbs.

16

A climber on **belay** is tied to a person on the ground with a rope. This helps keep the climber safe if he slips or falls.

A rock shelf called a **ledge** is a good place for rock climbers to rest and check their gear.

Many rock climbers **rappel** to get down a mountain. This climber has attached a rope to a rock and to her harness. She uses the rope to reach the ground.

Meet the Author

Jean Craighead George

Hobbies: Learning about different animals, swimming, listening to music

First pet: Turkey vulture

Fun fact: George's grandnephew, Scotty, was the model for the character Axel.

About this book: *Cliff Hanger* is the first title in a series of adventure books that feature Axel and Grits.

Other books: *Dear Katie, the Volcano Is a Girl; The Talking Earth; Vulpes the Red Fox*

Meet the Illustrator

Wendell Minor

Hobbies: Painting, being outdoors

Fun fact: Minor has illustrated more than 2000 book covers!

About this book: Before Minor illustrated *Cliff Hanger,* he traveled to Wyoming with Jean Craighead George. He climbed rocks and hiked.

Other books: *Abe Lincoln Remembers* (by Ann Turner), *Snow Bear* (by Jean Craighead George)

Internet

Visit Education Place and discover more about Jean Craighead George and Wendell Minor. **www.eduplace.com/kids**

JEAN CRAIGHEAD GEORGE
WENDELL MINOR

Cliff Hanger

Strategy Focus

The boy in this story takes a big risk to save his dog. Read carefully and try to **predict** what will happen next.

Axel washed his tin cup at the hand pump outside the Teton Mountains Climbing School hut and looked up. A storm cloud darkened Death Canyon. Lightning flashed. Axel was glad he wasn't rock climbing now.

"Axel!"

Two mountain climbers ran down the trail. "Your dog followed us up the mountain," one of the women said. "We had to leave him at the top of Cathedral Wall."

"You left Grits?" Axel was upset.

"That storm's bad," she said, looking over her shoulder. "We had to get out of there."

Axel's father, Dag, the leader of the school, heard the news.
He closed the registration book and stepped outside.

Lightning exploded.

Dag counted slowly.

"... thirty-eight, thirty-nine, forty ..."

Kaboom, drummed the thunder.

"A mile for every five counts," Dag said. "The storm's eight miles away. We've got enough time to get Grits."

Dag put on his belt, which jangled with climbing nuts and carabiners, [Kar-uh-BEE-nuhrs] and shouldered his rope and backpack.

Axel looked at his dad. "Thanks," he said, and put on his own mountain-climbing gear.

Axel and Dag trekked steadily up the wooded trails, climbed over rock avalanches, and finally arrived at the bottom of the shaft of rock that is Cathedral Wall. A lightning bolt split open the black cloud.

"One, two, three . . ."

Kaboom.

"The storm's only a half mile away," Dag said. "Too close. We'd better wait it out here."

From high on the wall came a howl. Axel looked up.

"Look! Grits got down to Monkey Ledge. If he tries to come on down, he'll fall. Let's go."

"No," said Dag. "We can't make that climb. It's too difficult. We'll go back to the trail split and up the ridge."

"That'll take too long," Axel said. "I can do it." He tied the rope to his belt and placed his foot in a crack. He reached up.

Dag had no choice. His son was climbing. He picked up the top coil of Axel's rope and took a deep breath.

"Think out your moves," he said, wrapping the rope around his waist and bracing his foot against a rock.

"On belay," he called out.

"Climbing!" Axel answered.

Axel climbed slowly, from crack to crack to ledge to crack, moving like a ballet dancer. His father let out rope as he climbed.

When Axel was fifteen feet up, he jammed a climber's nut securely into a crack. He clipped a carabiner into the nut, and his rope in the carabiner. He relaxed. If he fell now, the nut, the carabiner, and his dad would stop him from plunging to his death. He climbed on.

Axel looked up. Grits was crouched on the ledge, about to jump to him. "Stay!" Axel yelled.

Splats of rain hit the wall. Axel climbed very carefully. Using the tips of his fingers and the edges of his climbing shoes, he pulled himself upward until his hand found the rim of Monkey Ledge. The next move was dangerous. Climbers had fallen here.

Thinking clearly, Axel placed both hands firmly on the ledge and concentrated. Slowly he pressed on them. His body rose. When his arms were straight, he placed his right foot beside his right hand, then his left foot beside his left hand.

Bent like a hairpin, he found his balance and stood up. Grits wagged his tail but did not move. He was scared.

Lightning buzzed across the sky.

"One . . ."

KABOOM. Grits shivered.

"A quarter mile away."

Axel put a nut and carabiner in the wall and roped himself to them. He sat down beside Grits and breathed a sigh of relief. Grits was safe.

Axel picked up his little dog and hugged him.

The cloud opened, and rain poured down. Grits whimpered.

"It's all right," Axel whispered into his fur. "It's all right."

The sky flashed. *KABOOM!*

"No count," said Axel. "It's here, Grits. We're right in the center of the storm." Crackling electricity lifted the hair straight up on Axel's head and arms. The air hummed. Sparks snapped from his ears to the rocks.

He hugged Grits closer.

Flash.

". . . seven, eight, nine, ten . . ."

Kaboom.

"Two miles," said Axel. "The storm's going away."

Axel took a dog harness from his pocket and slipped it over Grits's head and shoulders.

The rain stopped. The sun came out. Axel picked up Grits and eased him over the edge of the ledge. Grits clawed the air.

"Dog on belay!" he called to his dad. Slowly Axel let out the rope, lowering Grits down through space.

"Got him!" Dag finally shouted, and looked up. "Axel," he shouted, "when you double your rope to rappel, you'll only have enough rope to get halfway down."

"I know it, but it's okay. I see a good ledge where the rope will end."

Axel wrapped the rope around an outcrop and clipped it to his harness. Then he put his back to the void and leaned out. Holding one end of the rope, letting out the other, he jumped out, dropped, caught himself, jumped out, dropped, caught himself.

And then he came to the end of the rope.

The planned route was still ten feet below.

Dag saw the problem. He studied the wall.

"If you can swing out to your left," he said quietly, "you'll find a good route."

Axel swung across the face of the wall. He reached but could not find a handhold near the route. He swung back. Dag foresaw a disaster.

"Stay where you are," he said. "I'm going for help."

"It'll be too dark," Axel answered. "I'll try again."

Axel ran like a track star back and forth across the vertical wall, back and forth. He swung wider and wider. When he was over Dag's route, he jammed his fist in a crack. He did not swing back.

Axel forced his toes into another crack. When he was secure and firmly balanced, he untied the rope from his waist, pulled it from the boulder on Monkey Ledge, and let it fall to his dad.

No nut, carabiner, or rope was there to save him if he made a mistake. From this moment on, he must free climb.

He began his descent.

Dag watched. The old pro said not one word, for fear of breaking his son's concentration.

When Axel was three feet from the ground, he whooped
and jumped down to his father.

"Did it!"

"That was so close, I can't talk about it," Dag said. There was
a flash in the canyon. Axel hugged Grits.

". . . twenty-one, twenty-two, twenty-thr — " *Kaboom!*

"The storm's at the hut," Dag said. "Let's wait it out here. I'm
beat." He lit his small gas stove and made soup with clear stream
water and instant mix. He poured some into a cup for Axel.

"I'll bet Grits sleeps well tonight," Dag said when he finally
relaxed. "He was one scared dog."

"I don't know about Grits," Axel answered. "But I was sure
scared. I thought I had lost my friend forever."

Think About the Selection

1. What makes *Cliff Hanger* an adventure? How does the author make you feel as if you are part of the adventure too?

2. Why do you think Axel isn't scared to go after Grits? What would you have done?

3. How would you describe the way Axel and his father feel about each other? What story details support your answer?

4. Read the first sentence on page 31 again. Why do you think the author compares Axel to a ballet dancer?

5. What would have happened to Grits if Axel had waited to start climbing until the storm had passed? Explain.

6. Connecting/Comparing How is *Cliff Hanger* like an adventure you have had? How is it different?

Describing

Write a Description

Axel clearly enjoys being outside. Write a description of a special outdoor place that you like to visit. Use details that will help someone who has never been to your place understand what it is like.

Tips

- Draw a picture of the place to help you remember details.
- Use words that describe what you see, hear, and smell.

Math

Write Word Problems

On pages 24 and 25, Dag counts the time between the flash of lightning and the boom of thunder. He says that for every five counts, the storm is one mile away. Now write three different word problems that ask how far away the storm is. Use skip counting to help you. Draw or write to explain each answer.

If I count to __40__, how far away is the storm?

__8__ miles

Listening and Speaking

Listen to Your World

Go back through the selection. Find all the sounds the author uses to describe the storm. Now open your ears! Choose a place, such as a park, a street corner, or your home. Listen carefully for five minutes. Write down what you hear.

Tips
- Stay quiet and still while you listen.
- Close your eyes to make listening easier.

Internet

Take an Online Poll

Have you ever gone hiking? Have you been rock climbing? Take an online poll at Education Place.

www.eduplace.com/kids

THESE KIDS ROCK

by Deborah Churchman
photos by Jackson Smith

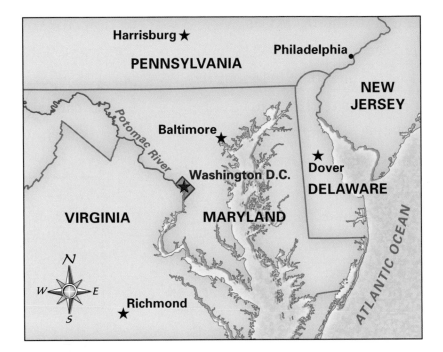

Harrisburg ★
PENNSYLVANIA
Philadelphia
NEW JERSEY
Potomac River
Baltimore ★
Dover ★
Washington D.C.
DELAWARE
VIRGINIA
MARYLAND
ATLANTIC OCEAN
N
W   E
S
Richmond ★

Maybe you've heard about adults climbing with ropes up steep cliffs and mountains. But is rock climbing for kids too?

You betcha. Just ask Camille, Magenta, Ed, and Tyler. Recently, these kids spent a day climbing the cliffs along the Potomac River near Washington, D.C. (see map). Helping them were guides from a company called SportRock.

The kids made climbing seem, well, not easy — but not impossible, either. Just look at Magenta. She proved that, with the right skills and equipment, kids can walk right up a cliff!

"Climbing takes more than just muscle," Magenta said. "It takes thinking and planning, too. Every time I climb, I learn something."

Suiting Up

The kids started by learning to put on their rope-climbing gear. First came the harness (what the rope attaches to). Like Camille, each kid had to practice figuring out all the harness straps. Why? Safety starts with knowing how to use your gear.

Next, the kids put on helmets to keep safe from falling rocks. Last, they put on sure-grip rock-climbing shoes. Then they were ready to go!

A Wild Beginning

The climb started on the riverbank at the bottom of a steep cliff. There, the kids saw all kinds of wild stuff going on. Turkey vultures soared overhead. Crows cawed. On the riverbank, Tyler even found some cool snail and clam shells.

Then the guides got the kids ready for *top-roping* — climbing with a rope that was anchored at the top of the cliff.

Climbing a Crack

The first thing to decide on a climb is which route to take up. Like many cliffs, this one had a crack running from top to bottom. A crack is a good — but tricky — place to climb.

Ed decided to try climbing the crack. He wedged his legs and toes into the corner and tucked his fingers wherever he could. Here's the big key to rock climbing: Most of the action is in the legs. So Ed used his leg muscles to push himself up. *Wedge, tuck, push. Wedge, tuck, push.* Robb, his guide, stood below and managed the rope as Ed went higher. You can make it, Ed!

Topping Off

Meanwhile, Tyler took a route up the cliff, straight up the wall. He tucked his feet and fingers into tiny holes and leaned back a little bit — just as if he were climbing a ladder. Far down below, Robb held the end of Tyler's rope.

And there he is, almost at the top of the cliff! He's grabbing the carabiner attached to the anchor ropes. Now he'll use his leg muscles to push himself up and over. Good job, Tyler!

Going Boulder

While Ed and Tyler did their top-roping, Magenta tried *bouldering* — climbing on big boulders. Bouldering is a good way to practice climbing without ropes. But it isn't easy. Here, Magenta uses her hands, thighs, and feet to grip and climb an overhang. Her guide, Jennifer, is "spotting" her to make sure she doesn't get hurt.

Time for Eats!

Finally, when everyone got to the top of the cliff, it was time for a BIG lunch and a look around. Then the kids got to *rappel* — go back down the cliff using the ropes. A guide managed the ropes while the kids "walked" right down the wall.

"Wow, that was *fun,*" said Tyler. "Can we do it again — please?"

A Personal Narrative

A personal narrative is a true story about something that happened to the writer. Use this student's writing as a model when you write a personal narrative of your own.

A good **beginning** makes the reader want to read on to find out what will happen.

Lost Shoes

Come on! Want to read about me losing my shoes? It was March 6, 1999. My friend Lindsey came over to play. She liked my shoes, and I liked hers, so we traded. A little later it was time for her to go home. I waved good-bye through my window as she walked away. The next morning my shoes were gone! I was as sad as a mother whose child is lost. Man, where could they be? I looked all over my room, but all I found was an old piece of pizza half eaten by ants. Ewwwww!

The first thing I did was to look through the whole house. But all I found was a dirty sock, 3 candy bars, an old map, and 15 pieces of paper. Next, I looked in the car but all I found was an old box,

50

6 watches, 7 candy wrappers, and a piece of cheese. I thought and looked and wondered where they could be.

Finally, I retraced my steps and remembered trading shoes with Lindsey. Then I zoomed to her house and asked for my shoes back. I was as relieved as a mother whose child has been found. I cleaned my shoes all day and man did they shine!

When I dressed for school the next day, I proudly tied the laces of my shiny blue shoes. I reached for my backpack but. . . . OH NO! WHERE'S MY BACKPACK???

Including **details** makes the narrative real for a reader.

It's important to keep to the **topic**.

A good **ending** pleases a reader.

Meet the Author

Nina M.

Grade: three
State: Florida
Hobbies: writing, reading, and playing with her sister
What she'd like to be when she grows up: an artist and musician

Background and Vocabulary

The Ballad of Mulan

Read to find the meanings of these words.

e ● Glossary

armor

comrades

endured

farewell

triumphant

troops

victorious

52

The Mulan Legend

An old Chinese legend tells the story of a young woman named Mulan. Many years ago, there was much war and fighting in China. China's leader, the Emperor, often drafted men to join the army. These men would say **farewell** to their families and leave home to serve with their **comrades**.

Sometimes the army would win a battle and return home **triumphant**. At other times, the men would not be **victorious**, even though they had bravely **endured** much hardship.

The old legend says that Mulan showed great courage during these difficult times. The story you are about to read retells the legend of how Mulan became a hero to the Chinese people.

These sculptures show how the Emperor's **troops** would put on **armor** to protect themselves.

This clay sculpture
shows what an army
horse might have
looked like.

This building sits on a cliff high above the Yellow River in
China, where the troops might have camped long ago.

MEET THE
AUTHOR AND ILLUSTRATOR
Song Nan Zhang

- Song Nan Zhang was born in Shanghai, China, in 1942.

- Once, when Mr. Zhang was a small child, he saw a baby tiger hiding in some plants outside his family's house. He ran into the kitchen and shouted, "Mom, Mom, there's a big cat outside!"

- As a young boy, Mr. Zhang drew some silly pictures of his father and hung them on a wall at home. Instead of getting angry, his father was proud that his son was such a good artist!

- Today, Mr. Zhang lives in Canada, where he works as an artist, author, and teacher.

OTHER BOOKS:

The Children of China
Cowboy on the Steppes

The Legend of the Panda
(by Linda Granfield)

The Man Who Made Paris
(by Frieda Wishinsky)

Internet

Learn more about Song Nan Zhang by visiting Education Place.

www.eduplace.com/kids

The Ballad of
MULAN
Retold by Song Nan Zhang

⭐ **Strategy Focus**

As you read, **monitor** how well you understand
the events in the story. Reread to **clarify** anything
that seems unclear.

木蘭辭　北朝樂府

不聞機杼聲惟聞女嘆息
唧唧復唧唧木蘭當戶織

Long ago, in a village in northern China, there lived a girl named Mulan. One day, she sat at her loom weaving cloth. *Click-clack! Click-clack!* went the loom.

女亦無所思 女亦無所憶
問女何所思 問女何所憶

木蘭辭　北朝樂府

Suddenly, the sound of weaving changed to sorrowful sighs.
"What troubles you?" her mother asked.
"Nothing, Mother," Mulan softly replied.

昨晚見軍帖可汗大點兵

木蘭辭　北朝樂府

Her mother asked her again and again, until Mulan
finally said, "There is news of war."

58

軍書十二卷卷卷有爺名

木蘭辭　北朝樂府

"Invaders are attacking. The Emperor is calling for troops. Last night, I saw the draft poster and twelve scrolls of names in the market. Father's name is on every one."

阿爺無大兒木蘭無長兄

木蘭辭　北朝樂府

"But Father is old and frail," Mulan sighed.
"How can he fight? He has no grown son and I have
no elder brother."

60

願為市鞍馬從此替爺征

木蘭辭　北朝樂府

"I will go to the markets. I shall buy a saddle and a horse. I must fight in Father's place."

東市買駿馬西市買鞍韉

木蘭辭　北朝樂府

From the eastern market Mulan bought a horse, and
from the western market, a saddle. From the southern market
she bought a bridle, and from the northern market, a whip.

南市買轡頭 北市買長鞭

木蘭辭

北朝樂府

At dawn Mulan dressed in her armor and bid a sad
farewell to her father, mother, sister, and brother. Then
she mounted her horse and rode off with the soldiers.

朝辭爺娘去暮宿黃河邊

木蘭辭　北朝樂府

By nightfall she was camped by the bank of
the Yellow River. She thought she heard her mother
calling her name.

64

但聞黃河流水鳴濺濺
不聞爺娘喚女聲

木蘭辭　北朝樂府

But it was only the sound of the river crying.

旦辭黃河去暮至黑山頭

木蘭辭　北朝樂府

At sunrise Mulan took leave of the Yellow River.
At dusk she reached the peak of Black Mountain.

但聞燕山胡騎聲啾啾

不聞爺娘喚女聲

木蘭辭

北朝樂府

In the darkness she longed to hear her father's voice but heard only the neighing of enemy horses far away.

萬里赴戎機關山度若飛

木蘭辭　北朝樂府

Mulan rode ten thousand miles to fight a hundred battles.
She crossed peaks and passes like a bird in flight.

朔氣傳金柝寒光照鐵衣

木蘭辭　北朝樂府

Nights at the camp were harsh and cold, but
Mulan endured every hardship. Knowing her father
was safe warmed her heart.

将军百战死

木蘭辭 北朝樂府

The war dragged on. Fierce battles ravaged the land.
One after another, noble generals lost their lives.

70

壮士十年歸

木蘭辞

北朝樂府

Mulan's skill and courage won her respect and rank. After ten years, she returned as a great general, triumphant and victorious!

歸来見天子天子坐明堂

木蘭辭　北朝樂府

The Emperor summoned Mulan to the High Palace.
He praised her for her bravery and leadership in battle.

策勳十二轉賞賜百千強

木蘭辭　北朝樂府

The Court would bestow many great titles upon her.
Mulan would be showered with gifts of gold.

木蘭辭 北朝樂府

木蘭不用尚書郎
可汗問所欲

"Worthy General, you may have your heart's desire,"
the Emperor said.

"I have no need for honors or gold," Mulan replied.

74

願借明駝千里足　送兒還故鄉

木蘭辭　北朝樂府

"All I ask for is a swift camel to take me back home."
The Emperor sent a troop to escort Mulan on her trip.

阿姊聞妹來當戶理紅妝
爺娘聞女來出廓相扶將

木蘭辭　北朝樂府

In town, the news of Mulan's return created great
excitement. Holding each other, her proud parents
walked to the village gate to welcome her.

76

小弟聞姊來　磨刀霍霍向豬羊

木蘭辭　北朝樂府

Waiting at home, Mulan's sister beautified herself.
Her brother sharpened his knife to prepare a pig and
sheep for the feast in Mulan's honor.

脱我戰時袍
著我舊時裳
開我東閣門
坐我西閣床

木蘭辭　北朝樂府

Home at last! Mulan threw open her bedroom door
and smiled. She removed her armor and changed into
one of her favorite dresses.

當窗理雲鬢對鏡貼花黃

木蘭辭　北朝樂府

She brushed out her shiny black hair and pasted
a yellow flower on her face. She looked into the
mirror and smiled again, happy to be home.

出門看伙伴
伙伴皆惊惶

木蘭辭

北朝樂府

What a surprise it was when Mulan appeared at
the door! Her comrades were astonished and amazed.
"How is this possible?" they asked.

同行十二年　不知木蘭是女郎

木蘭辭　北朝樂府

"How could we have fought side by side with you
for ten years and not have known you were a woman!"

雄兔腳撲朔雌兔眼迷離

木蘭辭　北朝樂府

Mulan replied, "They say the male rabbit likes to hop and leap, while the female rabbit prefers to sit still. But in times of danger, when the two rabbits scurry by, who can tell male from female?"

雙兔傍地走安能辨我是雄雌

木蘭辭 北朝樂府

Mulan's glory spread through the land. And to this day, we sing of this brave woman who loved her family and served her country, asking for nothing in return.

Think About the Selection

1. Why doesn't Mulan tell her mother right away that there is news of war?

2. What might have happened if Mulan had asked to fight dressed as a female soldier?

3. Why are the men who fought side by side with Mulan so surprised that she is a woman? List more than one reason.

4. What do Mulan's actions teach you about the meaning of courage?

5. The story of Mulan has been retold for hundreds of years. Why do you think people enjoy retelling it?

6. **Connecting/Comparing** Both Mulan and Axel in *Cliff Hanger* have tough jobs to do. How are the problems they face alike and different?

Write a Letter

May 23

Dear Father,

Mulan spent many nights away from home. Write a letter from Mulan to her father. Tell him what it's like where Mulan is and what she has been doing since she left home.

Tips

- **Use vivid words to describe people, places, and events.**
- **Remember to use the five parts of a letter.**

Make a Leadership Award

We know that Mulan was a good soldier. In a small group, discuss other ways Mulan was a good leader. Then discuss people who are good leaders in your community. Vote for the best leader. Make a leadership award for the winner. Write his or her name on the award.

Compare the Book and a Movie

Now that you've read *The Ballad of Mulan,* you may want to compare this version of the story to a movie version. Use a Venn diagram to list what is the same and what is different. Then choose one scene that was much better in either the movie or the book and discuss it with a classmate.

Internet

Post a Review

Tell other students around the country what you think of *The Ballad of Mulan*. Write a review of the story and post it on Education Place.

www.eduplace.com/kids

Language Link

Skill: How to Read a Key

A key is a chart that tells what symbols mean.

Before you read . . .

❶ **Look at** the key to see what information it gives you.

❷ **Predict** how you will use the key.

While you read . . .

❶ **Look back** at the key to match the symbols you find in the text.

❷ **Identify** the meaning of each symbol.

Chinese

Are you a 子 or a 女 or a 人? Do you wake with the 日 or the 月? Have you ever ridden in a 車 up a 山 in the 雨? Unless you read Chinese, you probably don't know the answers to these questions — yet!

Chinese writing is made up of pictures called characters. A long time ago, these pictures looked like the things they stood for. For example, ☉ was the picture for "sun," and ☽ was the picture for "moon." See the round sun and the half-moon? But over the centuries, the characters changed until they now look like 日 (sun) and 月 (moon). Imagine: over one billion people use this beautiful writing.

Read the story on page 89. See if you can figure out the meanings of the Chinese characters. The words and characters in the box will help you.

the Write Way

by Susan Wills
illustrated by
Lily Toy Hong

cart

child

fire

man

mountain

rain

sun

woman

moon

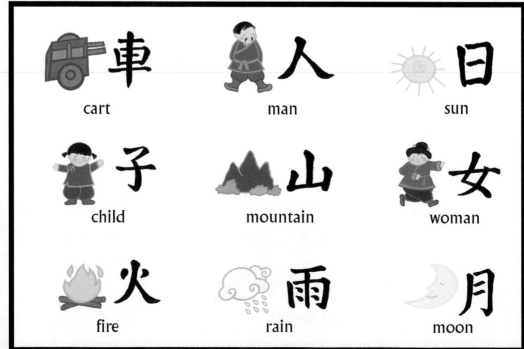

車 cart	人 man	日 sun
子 child	山 mountain	女 woman
火 fire	雨 rain	月 moon

On top of a 山 there lived a 人, a 女, and a 子. Every day when the 日 came up, they took their 車 and walked down the 山 to the market for food. Every night when the 月 rose, they walked back up the 山 to their home to eat supper.

After many years, the family grew very tired of all that walking up and down. "If only we had 雨 so that we could raise our own food," the 女 said.

Then one night, the 子 had a dream. The next morning when the 日 came up, the 子 went outside and started a 火 with some sticks. Since there had never been a 火 on top of the 山 before, the clouds were frightened and sent down 雨 to put the 火 out. From then on, anytime the family wanted 雨, one of them would start a small 火, and the clouds would hurry to put it out.

Soon the family had enough water to grow a fine vegetable garden. Of course, now the 子, the 女, and the 人 were all pretty tired of weeding vegetables and chasing rabbits from their garden. So one morning, when the 日 came up, they took their 車 and walked down the 山 to the market for food.

Now that you've read the story, why not make up your own tale using the same Chinese characters? When you've finished your tale, give it to a friend to read!

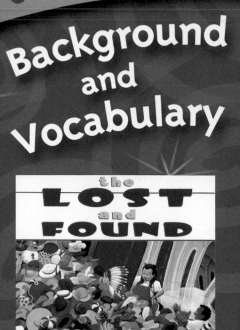
Have You Seen the Lost and Found?

If you've lost something in a store or at school, don't get **worried**. Just try asking for **directions** to the lost and found. A lost and found is a place to keep lost items until owners come to find them.

A visit to the lost and found can be an **unusual** adventure. Often the items are **visible** on shelves or tables. In other **situations**, the items may be tucked away in drawers or bins. Like the children in the story you are about to read, you may need to dig through piles of toys, shoes, or **rumpled** clothes to find what you're looking for. Be careful, though. You don't want to get lost yourself!

Lost
and
Found

Mark Teague

Mark Teague was always losing things when he was a kid. No surprise, then, that he often visited the lost and found at his school. He also thought that looking through the piles of lost toys and clothes was a lot of fun! Now you'll have a chance to see how Teague turned these real-life trips to the lost and found into an adventure story.

Other books:

Pigsty

Baby Tamer

The Secret Shortcut

How I Spent My Summer Vacation

Internet

Find out more about Mark Teague and his adventures by visiting Education Place.

www.eduplace.com/kids

the LOST and FOUND

mark teague

This adventure story has many twists and turns. When something surprising happens, stop and **summarize** to keep track of what you've read so far.

Wendell and Floyd were in trouble. That morning a giant
squid had trapped them in the boys' restroom for almost
an hour, causing them to miss a math test. Their teacher,
Ms. Gernsblatt, had been furious.

"We have no luck," said Floyd.

Just then, Mona Tudburn entered the office. Mona was the
new girl in their class.

"I'm trying to find the Lost and Found," she said. "I lost my lucky hat."

Wendell and Floyd glanced at each other. "That's strange," said Wendell. "We were just talking about luck."

"We don't have any," Floyd said.

"Neither do I," said Mona. "At least not without my hat."

95

Wendell pointed to a bin marked LOST AND FOUND. "I wish I had a lucky hat."

"So do I," Floyd agreed. "Then maybe we wouldn't get into these crazy situations."

Mona leaned farther and farther into the bin. Soon only her feet were visible. A moment later she was gone.

The boys walked over to have a closer look.
"Where did she go?" asked Wendell.
"I don't know," Floyd said. "She must be lost."
"Don't be silly," Wendell told him. "How can you get lost in the Lost and Found?"
Floyd looked at the principal's door and thought about all the trouble they would be in if they weren't there when they were called. "I guess we should go in after her," he sighed.

They climbed into the bin and instantly plunged into a
deep well of lost toys and clothing.

"Look, Floyd, we found Mona."
"I think I found you," Mona said.
"Maybe we should get back now," Floyd suggested.

Mona noticed a sign pointing to a narrow passageway.
HAT ROOM, it read. "I bet my hat's in there."

"It couldn't hurt to look," said Wendell.

"Wait," warned Floyd. "What if we get lost?"

But Wendell and Mona laughed. "You can't get lost
in the Lost and Found."

The passageway led to a cave where a deep lake gurgled and steamed. "I wonder if the principal knows this is here," said Floyd.

Wendell examined a suit of armor. "Some of this stuff has been lost a long time."

"I still don't see my hat," grumbled Mona.

Then Wendell found a boat. "Perfect! We'll paddle across."

On the far side of the lake were three tunnels. "Which way do we go now?" asked Floyd.

"We could flip a coin," Wendell suggested.

Mona frowned. "That only works if there are two choices. Here we have three."

The boys thought about that for a while. Finally Wendell threw up his hands. "Let's try the middle one."

The tunnel became a winding hallway full of doors. They opened each one without finding a single hat. "I knew we would get lost," Floyd muttered.

"You can't get lost in the Lost and Found," Mona and Wendell told him, but they no longer sounded so sure.

They came to one last door. Mona turned the knob and pulled . . .

"The Hat Room!" cried the boys.

But Mona shook her head in dismay. "There's too many! I'll never find my hat in here."

They decided to look anyway. "Is it this one?" asked Wendell. It wasn't.

"How about this one?" Floyd held up a huge pink hat with purple flowers and a canary.

"Of course not," said Mona.

The boys began trying on hats themselves. "How do you tell if one is lucky?" Floyd asked.

"I don't know," said Mona. "It'll just sort of feel lucky."

Wendell tried on a burgundy fez with a small gold tassel. "This one feels lucky."

While Floyd was finding his own lucky hat, Wendell's tassel began to tickle his nose. "I think I'm going to sneeze."

"Hold on. I'll get you a tissue." Mona reached into her purse, and when she did, a strange look came over her face. She held up something green and badly rumpled.

"My lucky hat. I guess it was in my purse all along."

For a moment, nobody spoke. Then Floyd sighed, "At least we can go back now."

"Maybe not," Wendell said.

"What do you mean?" asked Floyd and Mona.

"I mean, we might be lost."

Floyd groaned. "I thought you said we couldn't get lost in the Lost and Found."

"It's been an unusual day," said Wendell. "To be honest, I don't even remember which door we came through."

The children looked around. There were doorways in all directions. None of them could remember which one was theirs.

Suddenly Mona laughed. "What are we worried about? We've all got our lucky hats, right?"

She closed her eyes and turned slowly around. When she opened them again, she pointed straight ahead. "I say we go that way."

After a long journey, the children's heads popped out of the Lost and Found bin, just in time to hear the principal call, "Wendell and Floyd, come in here please."

It was late that afternoon before the boys left school.
They found their new friend Mona waiting for them.

"How was it?" she asked.

"Not bad," said Floyd.

The principal had merely lectured them about telling the truth. Of course, Ms. Gernsblatt had made them stay and finish their math tests, but it could have been worse.

"I think our luck is changing," said Wendell.

Mona nodded. "Me too."

Since it was late, they decided to take a shortcut.

"I hope we don't get lost," said Floyd, but he wasn't really worried. Neither were Mona and Wendell. They paused for a moment to put on their hats. Then they all started home, feeling lucky together.

Think About the Selection

1. Does luck have anything to do with Wendell and Floyd's troubles? Give reasons for your answer.

2. Why do the boys follow Mona into the Lost and Found bin?

3. Why do you think the world of the Lost and Found becomes stranger as the children go deeper into it?

4. What might have happened if the children hadn't gotten out of the Lost and Found when they did?

5. Would you have followed Mona into the Lost and Found? Why or why not?

6. **Connecting/Comparing** Which do you think is a more exciting adventure story, *The Ballad of Mulan* or *The Lost and Found*? Why?

Write Instructions

Now that you know the way, write step-by-step instructions for getting out of the Lost and Found. Start at the room right after the long fall through the Lost and Found bin.

Tips

- **Number the steps of your instructions.**
- **Use command words such as *turn* and *follow*.**

116

Work with Probability

Help the children choose one of the three tunnels. With a partner, make a spinner that gives each tunnel an equal chance of being picked. Spin it thirty times. Record how many times each tunnel comes up. Compare your results with the rest of the class.

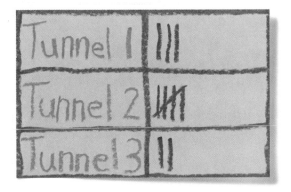

Bonus Make a spinner that gives one tunnel a greater chance of being picked than the other two. Spin it thirty times. Compare your results to the first thirty spins.

Draw a Room

Which room in *The Lost and Found* would you have liked to go into? Go back through the story. Choose a room you see there or create a new room that isn't shown in the illustrations. Draw the room and the things you might find in it.

Internet

Solve a Web Mystery Grid

Follow the instructions and find a picture that's been lost in the dots. Visit Education Place and print out a mystery grid.

www.eduplace.com/kids

Skill: How to Read a Poem

- **Read** the poem several times. Try reading the poem aloud.

- **Listen** for patterns, such as rhythm or rhyme.

- **Think** about the idea the poet is trying to express.

I Lost the Work I Found

Today
I lost
the
work
I found
in
the
lost
and
found
yesterday.

Tomorrow
in
the
lost
and
found
I'll find
the
work
I lost
today
after
I found
it
yesterday.

Kalli Dakos

Lost

I cannot find my basketball.
I cannot find my locker.
I cannot find my homework,
which is really quite a shocker.

I cannot find my lunch box.
Worse, I cannot find my classes.
I'm going to have a rotten day
until I find my glasses.

Bruce Lansky

September Yearning

Daddy hands me a shirt of many blues
And I've polished my sturdy shoes
And Mama's pressed my overalls
For the very first day of school falls
    in September

I reach for new books
And read about old heroes
I compute numbers
I calculate zeros

Then pages of poems I memorize
And paint the pictures
Behind my eyes

Joyce Carol Thomas

120

Check Your Progress

The adventures in this theme have taken you up cliffs, into ancient China, and through the lost and found. Now you will read and compare these adventures with two new selections. You will also practice your test-taking skills.

Look back at Mark Teague's letter on pages 13–14. Now that you've read about some adventures, what new ideas do you have about what every adventurer needs?

Get ready for two more great adventures! As you read, think about what makes each selection an adventure.

Read and Compare

A boy helps save a family from a hurricane.

Try these strategies:
Predict and Infer
Summarize

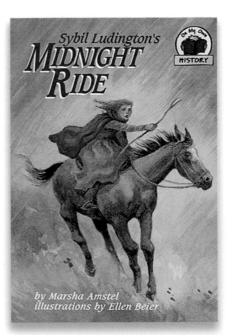

Read a true story about how a girl's horseback ride helped save her town.

Try these strategies:
Evaluate
Monitor and Clarify

Strategies in Action *Remember to use all your reading strategies while you read.*

RADIO RESCUE

written and illustrated by Lynne Barasch

In this story, which takes place in the 1920s, a boy operates a ham radio. From his shack, or home radio station, he sends and receives messages in Morse code. He taps out dots and dashes that stand for letters. Often the messages use shortened words. The boy is able to talk to other operators around the world using code names, such as 2AJC. He hopes one day to use his radio to help someone.

INTERNATIONAL MORSE CODE

A	·—		N	—·		1	·————
B	—···		O	———		2	··———
C	—·—·		P	·——·		3	···——
D	—··		Q	——·—			
E	·		R	·—·		4	····—
F	··—·		S	···		5	·····
G	——·		T	—		6	—····
H	····		U	··—			
I	··		V	···—		7	——···
J	·———		W	·——		8	———··
K	—·—		X	—··—		9	————·
L	·—··		Y	—·——		0	—————
M	——		Z	——··			

In 1926, a ferocious hurricane struck the Florida coast, wiping out all the phone lines. Ham radio operators have always been on the job in emergencies. Often they are the first to pick up distress calls. The Coast Guard radio was completely tied up handling local rescue operations, leaving ham radio as the only way for outsiders to get news from the disaster area.

I sat glued to my receiver, listening to traffic, when I picked up a message from 4LDG in Miami. 4LDG was transmitting the names of people who had survived the storm and wanted to tell family and friends in New York that they were safe.

I carefully wrote down all the names to call, thinking that was the end of the message. But it wasn't. Just as I was ready to sign off, I heard FAMILY STRANDED IN FLOOD ON KEY LARGO QSB (SIGNAL FADING) PLES CALL COAST GUARD, and he signed off.

I tried to raise the Coast Guard on ordinary channels but couldn't get through. I kept thinking about the family on Key Largo. Maybe they had a boy like me, maybe a dog like mine. Maybe they were huddled on the roof of a house waiting for a rescue. I got on the emergency band reserved for official use and sent: SOS FAMILY STRANDED ON KEY LARGO EXACT LOCATION UNKNOWN SEND HELP RUSH. I sent that message over and over.

Finally the Coast Guard in Miami acknowledged. It would send a boat out to look for the family.

I stayed on the air most of the night relaying more hurricane news until finally the Coast Guard in Miami broke in with FAMILY ON KEY LARGO SAFE TKS TO U. In spite of my excitement, I signed off and went to sleep. I had been working traffic for twenty-four hours!

A few days later, a reporter came to interview me and take a picture of me and my shack. The newspaper headline said:

INFANT RADIO OPERATOR TALKS TO TWELVE
FOREIGN STATIONS NIGHTLY

I wasn't too happy about being called an infant, and there was no mention of the hurricane rescue, but I didn't mind. We ham radio operators like nothing better than to help whenever there is a disaster. I was proud to be a small part of that great tradition.

Sybil Ludington's MIDNIGHT RIDE

by Marsha Amstel
illustrated by Neal Armstrong

In 1777, Americans were at war with the British. When British troops attacked a small town in Connecticut, the American commander, Colonel Ludington, had a problem. His soldiers had gone home to plant their crops. It was up to the Colonel's daughter, Sybil, to call the Americans back into battle.

The rain was steady and hard. Only a mile from home, raindrops started to seep through Sybil's cloak. Her hair was soaked. Rain ran down her face.

Then Sybil saw a flicker of candlelight through the darkness. It was the first farmhouse on her route. She slowed Star to a trot and banged on the door with her stick.

"The British are burning Danbury!" she shouted. "Meet at Colonel Ludington's house!" Then she urged Star on, back into the dark woods. She had no time to waste.

Sybil stopped at house after house. She stayed just long enough to call out her message and listen for an answer. Then she would ride on into the night.

The cold rain made Sybil's teeth chatter. Her fingers felt stiff on the reins. She woke so many families that she lost count.

As she rode toward the village of Carmel, she saw a strange orange glow in the eastern sky. It was the light from the fires of Danbury, twenty miles away. Sybil thought about how she would feel if her own home were burning. "We must hurry, Star," she whispered.

Sybil knew that she did not have to knock at every door. Neighbors would run to tell one another. They would make sure that all the soldiers heard the news.

Sybil rode into Carmel, calling out her message. Doors flew open at the sound of her shouts. As she rode away, the bell on the meetinghouse rang out. The bell would wake the townspeople and call them to action.

Sybil Ludington was able to warn her father's soldiers about the British attacks. The Americans marched, took the British by surprise, and forced them back to their ships.

Think and Compare

1. Sybil Ludington and the boy from *Radio Rescue* have reasons for helping other people. Compare the reasons. How are the reasons alike or different?

2. How do Axel and Mulan both show that they are brave? Give at least two examples.

3. Which two characters in this theme do you think are most alike or different? Explain.

4. Which adventure in the theme would you most like to be a part of? Why?

Strategies in Action Explain how you used a reading strategy while reading one of the selections.

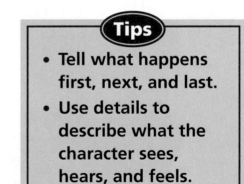

Reflecting

Write a Journal Entry

Choose a character from one of the selections in this theme. Write a journal entry that the character might write about the adventure. What was the scariest part? Which part was the most fun or exciting?

Tips
- Tell what happens first, next, and last.
- Use details to describe what the character sees, hears, and feels.

Choosing the Best Answer

Some test questions have three or four answer choices. For these types of tests, you need to choose the best answer. A test about *Radio Rescue* might have this question.

Read the question. Fill in the circle next to the best answer.

1 What is the first thing the boy does when he can't raise the Coast Guard on the radio?

○ He signs off.

○ He tells a reporter about the emergency.

● He sends a message on the emergency band.

○ He listens to traffic on his ham radio.

 Understand the question.

Find the key words.
Use them to understand
what you need to do.

> I think the key words are *first, raise,* and *Coast Guard.* I need to figure out what the boy did first after trying to reach the Coast Guard.

Look back at the selection.

Think about where to find the answer. You may need to look in more than one place. Use the key words to skim the selection.

> I should go to the part where the boy gets the message about the family. That's when the boy tries to reach the Coast Guard.

 Narrow the choices. Then choose the best answer.

Find the choices that are clearly wrong. Have a good reason for choosing an answer. Guess only if you have to.

> The first and second choices are wrong because they happen toward the end of the story. The fourth choice happens too early. The third choice is the answer.

POETRY

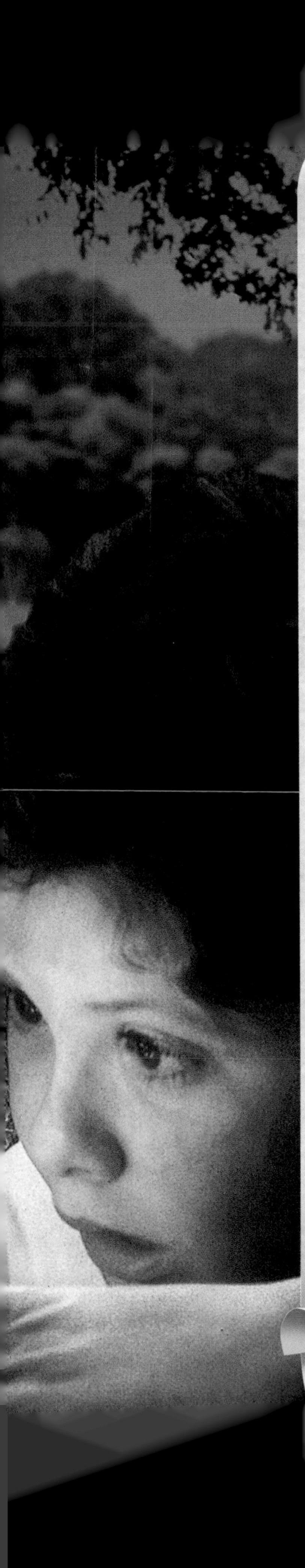

Poetry

Poems can create songs
without music,
pictures without paint,
and feelings with
just a few words.

A poem describes things, shares
a feeling, and tells a story.
A poem has a **rhythm**, or pattern
of beats, like a song.

A poem may be made of parts,
or **stanzas**. The words in a
poem may make a shape.

A poem's words may **rhyme** —
but not all the time.
Turn the page to see and hear
what poems do!

Focus on Genre

Contents

April Rain Song

Let the rain kiss you.
Let the rain beat upon your head with silver liquid drops.
Let the rain sing you a lullaby.

The rain makes still pools on the sidewalk.
The rain makes running pools in the gutter.
The rain plays a little sleep-song on our roof at night —

And I love the rain.

by Langston Hughes

Sneeze

There's a
sort of a
tickle
the size of a
nickel,
a bit like the
prickle
of sweet-sour
pickle;

it's a
quivery
shiver
the shape of a
sliver,
like eels in a
river;

a kind of a
wiggle
that starts as a
jiggle
and joggles
its way to a
tease,

which I
cannot
suppress
any longer,
I guess,
so pardon me,
please,
while I
sneeze.

by Maxine Kumin

JOE

We feed the birds in winter,
And outside in the snow
We have a tray of many seeds
For many birds of many breeds
And one gray squirrel named Joe.
    But Joe comes early,
    Joe comes late,
    And all the birds
    Must stand and wait.
And waiting there for Joe to go
Is pretty cold work in the snow.

by David McCord

Cloud Dragons

What do you see
in the clouds so high?
What do you see in the sky?

Oh, I see dragons
that curl their tails
as they go slithering by.

What do you see
in the clouds so high?
What do you see? Tell me, do.

Oh, I see *caballitos*
that race the wind
high in the shimmering blue.

by Pat Mora

giraffe

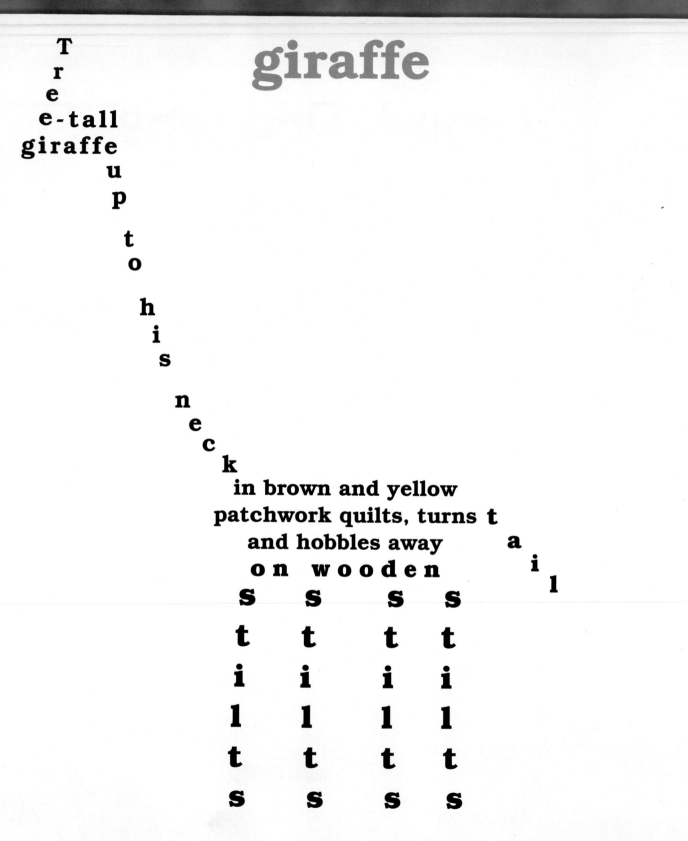

Tree-tall giraffe up to his neck in brown and yellow patchwork quilts, turns tail and hobbles away on wooden stilts stilts stilts stilts

by J. Patrick Lewis

144

Spaghetti! Spaghetti!

Spaghetti! spaghetti!
You're wonderful stuff,
I love you spaghetti,
I can't get enough.
You're covered with sauce
and you're sprinkled with cheese,
spaghetti! spaghetti!
oh, give me some please.

Spaghetti! spaghetti!
piled high in a mound,
you wiggle, you wriggle,
you squiggle around.
There's slurpy spaghetti
all over my plate,
spaghetti! spaghetti!
I think you are great.

Spaghetti! spaghetti!
I love you a lot,
you're slishy, you're sloshy,
delicious and hot.
I gobble you down
oh, I can't get enough,
spaghetti! spaghetti!
you're wonderful stuff.

by Jack Prelutsky

145

ANDRE

I had a dream last night. I dreamed
I had to pick a Mother out.
I had to choose a Father too.
At first, I wondered what to do,
There were so many there, it seemed,
Short and tall and thin and stout.

But just before I sprang awake,
I knew what parents I would take.

And this surprised and made me glad:
They were the ones I always had!

by Gwendolyn Brooks

The Bat

The bat is batty as can be.
It sleeps all day in cave or tree,
And when the sun sets in the sky,
It rises from its rest to fly.
All night this mobile mammal mugs
A myriad of flying bugs.
And after its night out on the town,
The batty bat sleeps

Upside down.

by Douglas Florian

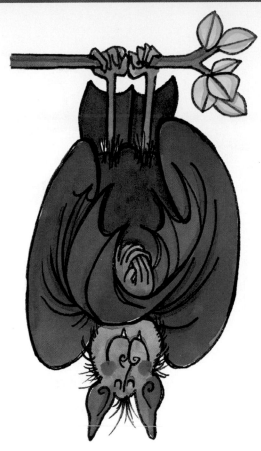

If I Were an Ant

Suppose I
were an ant —
I'd be lazy
for sure.
And
I wouldn't save my food —
I'd eat lots.

by Hitomi Takeshi

Books

oversized
passports

that let us
travel

anywhere
anytime

and keep on
dreaming

Los libros

pasaportes
de talla mayor

que nos permiten
viajar

a dondequiera
cuandoquiera

y no dejar
de soñar

by Francisco X. Alarcón

SHOW FISH

I found a flounder and I thought, "*Swell,*
I'll take it to school for show and tell."
But I forgot, for quite a spell,
To take it to school for show and tell,
And now it's two weeks later. . . . Well . . .
I'll take it to school for show and *smell*.

by Shel Silverstein

Think About the
POETRY

1. "Joe" and "giraffe" both show the reader an animal. Compare the way the two poems do this.

2. The poets who wrote "Spaghetti! Spaghetti!" and "Books" describe their feelings about these two topics. Do you agree with the poets? Why or why not?

3. How do "April Rain Song" and "Cloud Dragons" help the reader see, hear, and feel nature?

4. Which poem did you like the best? Why?

Send an E-Postcard

How did you like the poems? Send an e-postcard to a friend. Tell your friend about some of the poems you have enjoyed. You can find the postcard at Education Place. **www.eduplace.com/kids**

Creating

Write a Poem

What will your poem be about? It can be about anything — a special person, an event, or a pet. Your poem can be happy, sad, or silly. How will your poem sound? You may want the poem to rhyme or have a special rhythm. Just start writing and see how your poem takes shape.

Tips

- Think about your topic. Then make a list of words that go with your topic. Write colorful words that help a reader feel, see, smell, or hear.

- Set your poem aside for a day or two after you write it. Then read your poem aloud to hear if it says what you want it to.

Celebrating Traditions

The town I live in, the street,
the house, the room,
The pavement of the city,
or a garden all in bloom,
The church, the school,
the clubhouse,
The million lights I see,
but especially the people —
That's America to me!

from the song
"The House I Live In"
lyrics by Lewis Allan

Celebrating Traditions

with Patricia Polacco

Dear Ones,

None of us would have traditions if we hadn't been told of them by our elders. It is through them and their stories that we all have a sense of who we are and where we come from. I most certainly would not be an author today if I hadn't come from a family of glorious storytellers.

One of our family stories is about this handmade quilt.

154

This is me with my brother Rich and my dad.

Gramma and Grampa Barber

When I was very young my parents divorced, and both of them moved back into their parents' homes. My brother and I had the glory of living with our grandparents, who loved to tell wonderful stories. During the summer, we lived with our dad. From Gramma and Grampa Barber, we heard about the Banshee, the Pooka, and the Costabower.

This is my mom as a baby with Gramma Gaw.

During the school year, my brother and I lived with our mother. Evening stories were the sweetest part of the day. Gramma Gaw would poke the fire in the fireplace, pop popcorn, and wedge apples. Then she would trundle back into the living room with the food and nestle in front of the fire.

Gramma Gaw's eyes blazed as she told us stories of the dreaded BaBaYaGa, Mother Frost, and Vasalissa and the Wolves. My brother and I leaned into her, shoveling popcorn into our gaping mouths. Her voice washed through us. We'd interrupt and ask for parts of the stories to be told over again. Gramma Gaw called this "firetalking."

What I remember most about firetalking is how it made me feel. I knew that I was loved by folks that were worlds away, from another time. The same feeling is in each of the selections in this theme. As you read, you'll see how traditions can show people who they are.

Enjoy the traditions,

Patricia Polacco

my mom and me

156

Let's Celebrate!

Patricia Polacco says in her letter that storytelling was an important tradition in her family. What traditions does your family have that are important to you?

Look at the selection covers pictured below. What types of traditions do you think you'll read about in this theme? As you read the selections, think about how the characters feel about their family traditions.

Are you ready to listen to some salsa music? Are you ready to dance with the Tewa? Then let's begin!

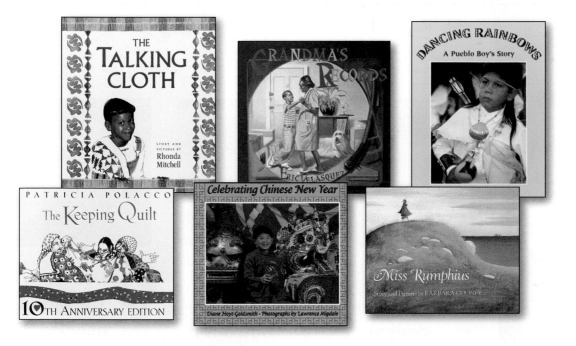

Internet

To learn about the authors in this theme, visit Education Place. **www.eduplace.com/kids**

PATRICIA POLACCO

The Keeping Quilt

10TH ANNIVERSARY EDITION

The Keeping Quilt

**Read to find
the meanings
of these words.**

e ● Glossary

border

gathering

needles

scraps

sewn

threaded

Quilts

A quilt is made of two layers of cloth **sewn** together using **needles** and thread. Quilt makers often use **scraps** of colorful old clothing to create designs. Sometimes they use large scraps to make a **border** around the edges of the quilt.

Many families have homemade quilts. Some families bring out their quilts only for a family **gathering**, such as a wedding or a birthday. Other people use their quilts every day. A family quilt, like the one in the selection you are about to read, helps people remember special times. It keeps them warm, inside and out.

1 **Cut out shapes or designs.**

2 **Attach beads or buttons if you like.**

3 **Use threaded needles to sew on the shapes.**

4 Enjoy your
finished quilt.

Patricia Polacco

 When Patricia Polacco was a child her family spent many hours telling stories. Listening to them made Polacco want to share these wonderful stories with others. One of her favorite things to tell young writers is "LISTEN . . . LISTEN . . . LISTEN."

After college, Polacco lived in Australia, England, France, Russia, and California. Now Polacco lives on a farm in Michigan with her husband, her cats, two goats, and a lamb. Her grown children live about forty miles away and visit often.

Other Books

Chicken Sunday

My Rotten Redheaded Older Brother

Luba and the Wren

Thank You, Mr. Falker

Internet

There's more to learn about Patricia Polacco on Education Place. **www.eduplace.com/kids**

PATRICIA POLACCO

The Keeping Quilt

10TH ANNIVERSARY EDITION

Strategy Focus

As you read, **evaluate** how well Patricia Polacco helps you understand her feelings about her family's quilt and their traditions.

When my Great-Gramma Anna came to America, she wore the same thick overcoat and big boots she had worn for farm work. But her family weren't dirt farmers anymore. In New York City, her father's work was hauling things on a wagon, and the rest of the family made artificial flowers all day.

Everyone was in a hurry, and it was so crowded, not like backhome Russia. But all the same it was their home, and most of their neighbors were just like them.

When Anna went to school, English sounded to her like pebbles dropping into shallow water. *Shhhhhh ... Shhhhhh ... Shhhhhh.* In six months she was speaking English. Her parents almost never learned, so she spoke English for them, too.

The only things she had left of backhome Russia were her dress and babushka she liked to throw up into the air when she was dancing.

And her dress was getting too small. After her mother
had sewn her a new one, she took her old dress and babushka.
Then from a basket of old clothes she took Uncle Vladimir's shirt,
Aunt Havalah's nightdress, and an apron of Aunt Natasha's.

"We will make a quilt to help us always remember home,"
Anna's mother said. "It will be like having the family in backhome
Russia dance around us at night."

And so it was. Anna's mother invited all the neighborhood ladies. They cut out animals and flowers from the scraps of clothing. Anna kept the needles threaded and handed them to the ladies as they needed them. The border of the quilt was made of Anna's babushka.

On Friday nights Anna's mother would say the prayers that started the Sabbath. The family ate challah and chicken soup. The quilt was the tablecloth.

Anna grew up and fell in love with Great-Grandpa Sasha. To show he wanted to be her husband, he gave Anna a gold coin, a dried flower, and a piece of rock salt all tied into a linen

handkerchief. The gold was for wealth, the flower for love, and the salt so their lives would have flavor.

She accepted the hankie and they were engaged.

Under the wedding huppa, Anna and Sasha promised each other love and understanding. After the wedding, the men and women celebrated separately.

When my Grandma Carle was born, Anna wrapped her daughter in the quilt to welcome her warmly into the world. Carle was given a gift of gold, flower, salt, and bread. Gold so she would never know poverty, a flower so she would always know love, salt so her life would always have flavor, and bread so that she would never know hunger.

Carle learned to keep the Sabbath and to cook and clean and do washing.

"Married you'll be someday," Anna told Carle, and . . .

again the quilt became a wedding huppa, this time for Carle's wedding to Grandpa George. Men and women celebrated together, but they still did not dance together. In Carle's wedding bouquet were a gold coin, bread, and salt.

Carle and George moved to a farm in Michigan and Great-Gramma Anna came to live with them. The quilt once again wrapped a new little girl, Mary Ellen.

Mary Ellen called Anna, Lady Gramma. She had grown very old and was sick a lot of the time. The quilt kept her legs warm.

On Anna's ninety-eighth birthday, the cake was a kulich, a rich cake with raisins and candied fruit in it.

When Great-Gramma Anna died, prayers were said to lift her soul to heaven. My mother Mary Ellen was now grown up.

When Mary Ellen left home, she took the quilt with her. When she became a bride, the quilt became her huppa. For the first time, friends who were not Jews came to the wedding. My mother wore a suit, but in her bouquet were gold, bread, and salt.

The quilt welcomed me, Patricia, into the world . . . and it was the tablecloth for my first birthday party.

At night, I would trace my fingers around the edges of each animal on the quilt before I went to sleep. I told my mother stories about the animals on the quilt. She told me whose sleeve had made the horse, whose apron had made the chicken, whose dress had made the flowers, and whose babushka went around the edge of the quilt.

The quilt was a pretend cape when I was in the bullring, or sometimes a tent in the steaming Amazon jungle.

At my wedding, men and women danced together. In my bouquet were gold, bread, and salt — and a sprinkle of grape juice, so I would always know laughter.

Many years ago I held Traci Denise in the quilt for the first time.

Three years later my mother held Steven John in the quilt for the first time. We were all so proud of Traci's new baby brother.

Just like their mother, grandmother, and great-grandmother before them, they, too, used the quilt to celebrate birthdays and make superhero capes.

As the years passed and Traci and Steven were growing up, their grandmother took pleasure at every family gathering to tell the story of the quilt. We all knew whose clothes made each flower and animal. My mother was lucky enough to show the wonder of this quilt to my brother's grandchildren, her great-grandchildren.

When my mother died, prayers were said to lift her soul to heaven. Traci and Steven were now all grown up and getting ready to start their own lives.

And now I wait . . . for the day that I, too, will be a grandmother, and tell the story of the Keeping Quilt to my grandbabies.

Think About the Selection

 1. Why does Anna's mother start the tradition of the Keeping Quilt?

2. Compare each daughter's wedding to her mother's wedding. How is each wedding different and the same?

3. How do you think Patricia Polacco feels about her family? Give examples from the story.

4. What does the Keeping Quilt help the family keep? In what other ways might a family keep something?

5. Why do you think Polacco has drawn only part of each illustration in color?

6. **Connecting/Comparing** How does this story help you understand traditions and what they mean to families?

Narrating

Write a Story

You know how Patricia Polacco feels about the Keeping Quilt. How would the quilt's story be different if the quilt were telling it? What parts would be the same? Write the quilt's version of the Polacco family history.

Tips
- Make a story map to help you remember people and events.
- Look closely at the illustrations for ideas.

Make a Family Tree

Draw the Polacco family tree. At the top of it, write the names of the oldest family members. List husbands and wives beside each other. Then write children's names below their parents. Draw lines to connect relatives. Look back at the story as you work.

Make a Class Keeping Quilt

Celebrate the year with a paper Keeping Quilt. Create a quilt square that shows a favorite event, person, or place. Then make a class quilt from the squares. You can add to it all year long.

Complete a Web Crossword Puzzle

Take a vocabulary challenge! Print a crossword puzzle about *The Keeping Quilt* from Education Place.

www.eduplace.com/kids

Nesting Dolls

by Marie E. Kingdon

Have you ever seen a nesting or stacking doll? A nesting doll is brightly painted, made of wood, and opens into two parts — a top and a bottom.

Do you know why they are called "nesting" dolls? When you open the first doll, there's another doll nested inside. Sometimes there are two or three dolls inside. Sometimes there are five or even ten or more. Guess how many are in the largest nesting doll we know about in the world? Would you believe, seventy-two! The largest doll in that set is three feet tall.

When you open each doll, there's another doll nested inside.

Some of the first nesting dolls were made in China a very, very long time ago — some say even a thousand years. Today nesting dolls are made in Poland, China, the Netherlands, India, and even the United States of America. But the best and the prettiest are made in Russia, where they are called "Matryoshkas" [maht-ree-OSH-kahs]. This comes from a common name for women in Russian country villages, "Mastryona," [mahst-ree-OH-nah] or village mother. Nesting, or Matryoshka, dolls are often given as gifts to new babies in Russia.

Some nesting dolls have a whole family inside: father, mother, sister, brother. Some Matryoshkas open and have ten solid dolls, all the same size, inside. These are called "counting Matryoshkas" because they help Russian children learn to count.

Here is a family of nesting dolls.

Matryoshka dolls made in Russia come from different regions, just as different products come from different states in America. Nesting, or Matryoshka, dolls are hand-painted and are dressed in costumes from the region where they are made. Some wear aprons and kerchiefs or scarves. Some hold flowers or baskets. The most common dolls are brightly painted in reds and yellows and have many coats of lacquer to protect them. Other dolls are painted in greens, blues, pastels, and even gold metallic.

A very fine set of dolls from Russia might have a different scene from a fairy tale on each doll in the series. These dolls tell a story with pictures, not words.

Nesting dolls are pretty, and they are great for play. Some children even have collections of different nesting dolls. These dolls can be fun for everyone. Tell your friends what you have learned about Matryoshkas. Have fun looking at and playing with these interesting, unique, wooden dolls.

Instructions

The purpose of writing instructions is to tell others how to do or make something. Use this student's writing as a model when you write instructions of your own.

Titles for instructions usually tell what the writing is about.

How to Have a Great Thanksgiving

My favorite celebration is on Thanksgiving.

I really like Thanksgiving because of all the stuff

that we do together. If you want to have a great

Thanksgiving like mine, here's how to do it.

Topic sentences make a good **beginning** for a piece of writing.

First, wake up in the morning and take a

deep breath. Smell the turkey cooking and the

sweet potatoes baking.

Then go downstairs to the living room and

watch the Thanksgiving parade on TV. Look for all

the GREAT floats and BIG balloons. You'll really like it. I wait all year just to watch the parade.

After that, it's the afternoon. You should invite your whole family over to enjoy the tasty dinner. Everyone at our house eats, talks, and then watches the football game.

If you follow these steps, you will have a great Thanksgiving just like mine.

Good instructions have **sequence words,** such as *first, then,* and *after that.*

It is important to make sure that directions are **complete**.

Meet the Author

Jamie S.

Grade: three

State: New York

Hobbies: playing school

What she'd like to be when she grows up: a teacher

Salsa Music

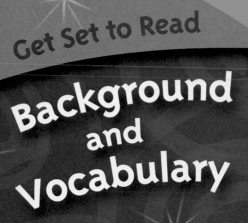

Grandma's Records

Read to find
the meanings
of these words.

e • Glossary

conga
percussion
performing
record
salsa
theater

Have you ever heard of a kind of music called **salsa**? Imagine that you are walking into a **theater**. On stage a salsa band is **performing**. The sounds fill the building.

You can hear trumpets and saxophones mixing their sounds with a piano and violin. Drums and other **percussion** instruments make the floor shake. People in the crowd are dancing and singing along with the band.

maracas

timbale

conga

Watching a band play live can be a lot of fun. But if you can't go to a concert, you can still enjoy your favorite band. Just play a **record**, a tape, or a CD!

Meet the Author and Illustrator

Eric Velasquez

As a child, Eric Velasquez was always doodling and sketching. His parents and grandmother kept sketchbooks, paints, and crayons around the house to keep him busy. Velasquez loved reading comic books, and he started creating his own.

Velasquez's first job as an illustrator was painting book covers. As he grew older, Velasquez realized that he missed the stories in his comic books. So Velasquez started to illustrate the stories in books, not just book covers.

Velasquez likes to listen to music while he works. After Velasquez finished *Grandma's Records*, he began listening to more and more Latin music.

Other books Velasquez has illustrated:

David Gets His Drum (by David Francis and Bob Reiner)

Champion: The Story of Muhammad Ali (by James Haskins)

The Sound That Jazz Makes (by Carole Boston Weatherford)

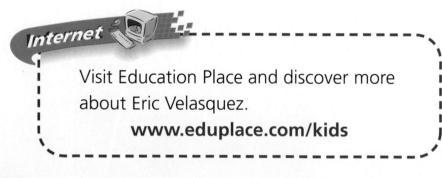

Internet

Visit Education Place and discover more about Eric Velasquez.

www.eduplace.com/kids

GRANDMA'S RECORDS

ERIC VELASQUEZ

Strategy Focus

As you read this story, think of **questions** about the boy, his grandmother, and their traditions that you would like to discuss later.

Every year, right after the last day of school, I'd pack a suitcase with my cool summer clothes, my favorite toys, and a sketchbook. Then my dog, Daisy, and I were off to Grandma's apartment in El Barrio. Because my parents worked, Grandma's apartment was my summer home.

From the time my parents dropped me off until the day they picked me up, Grandma wrapped me in her world of music.

Sometimes when she played a record, we would dance together. Other times, she would dance alone and tell me her stories about growing up in Puerto Rico.

When Grandma played a merengue from the Dominican Republic, her hips would sway from side to side. As her favorite salsa record played, she'd say, "Just listen to that conga," while she played an imaginary drum.

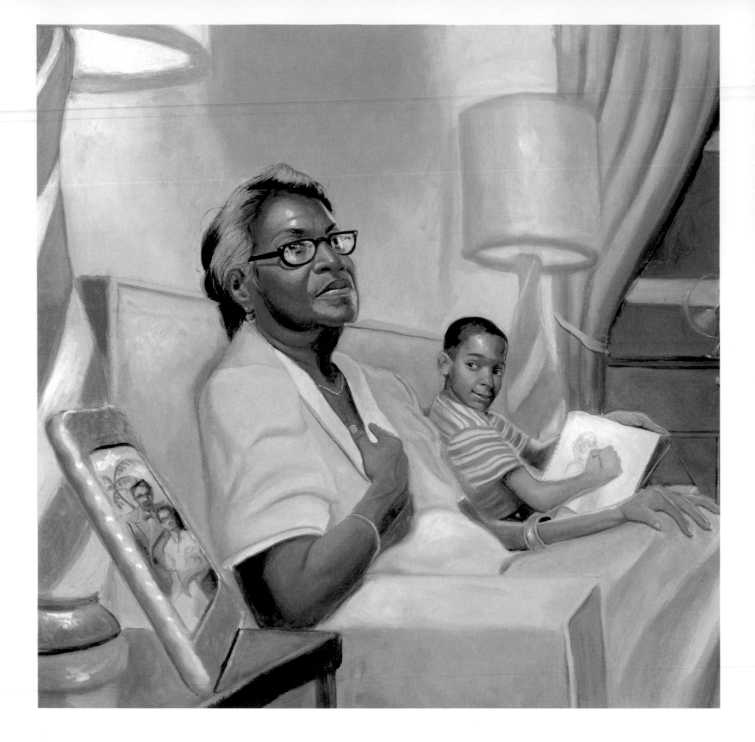

Grandma liked all types of music. But one record was very special to her. Whenever she played it, she would put her hand over her heart and close her eyes as she sang along. When it was over, Grandma would sometimes sit quietly, thinking about Grandpa and the old days in Santurce, her hometown.

"Sometimes," Grandma said, "a song can say everything that is in your heart as if it was written just for you."

My favorite days were the ones when Grandma would tell me, "You pick the records today." No matter what I would choose, Grandma would always say, *"Siempre me gusta tu selección."* (I always like your selection.)

Sometimes I would sneak in Grandma's special song just to watch her put her hand over her heart and sing.

Then she'd always ask, *"¿Cómo tú sabes?"* (How did you know?)

If it was too hot to go outside, I'd spend hours looking
through all of Grandma's album covers. I'd pick out my
favorites and make sketches of the art. As I drew, I could see
the record covers coming to life and the bands performing right
there in Grandma's living room.

Grandma never went to any nightclubs to see her
favorite bands perform. She was happy just to stay home with
me and listen to her scratchy records. But Santurce was home
to hundreds of musicians, and she knew a lot of the people
who played on the records.

Grandma's nephew Sammy played percussion in Rafael Cortijo's band, the best band in Puerto Rico. One day when the band was in town, Sammy brought over Cortijo and the band's lead singer, Ismael Rivera, for a surprise visit. Home-cooked meals were hard to come by on the road, and they couldn't pass up the chance to taste Grandma's famous *arroz con gandules* (rice and pigeon peas).

While eating dessert, Sammy had another surprise for Grandma: two tickets to the band's first New York concert, and their brand-new record, which wasn't even in the stores yet. I raced over to the record player, thrilled to be the first New Yorker to hear their latest music.

The next day, Grandma and I spent all day shopping for clothes to wear to the show. She even made me get a haircut.

The theater was all the way up in the Bronx. We took the subway there, and Grandma was nervous during the whole ride. When we got to the theater, we walked past the long line of people and went right inside because of our special tickets. The theater was bigger than all the movie theaters I had ever gone to.

The band made a spectacular entrance. Suddenly the theater went dark, tiny lights glittered, and a loud siren filled the air.

I heard Grandma gasp, "*¡Ay, Dios mío!*" (Oh my god). She thought something was wrong.

The darkened stage seemed to fill with people running back and forth in confusion. Next, everything went dark again, and a loud and steady conga beat began BOOM BAK BOOM BAK BOOM BAK. Then the lights came on with a loud BOOM, and the band began to play the song "*El Bombón de Elena*" ("Elena's Candy").

Grandma and I were surprised at how different the music sounded live. The musicians made familiar songs sound fresh by adding new musical phrases and words.

Before the last song began, Ismael said, "This one goes out to Carmen," and he pointed to Grandma as he sang her special song.

I looked at her as she put her hand over her heart, raised the other hand, closed her eyes, and began to sing along. Ismael was singing to my grandma! Then I looked around and realized that everyone in the theater had their hands over their hearts too.

After the show we went backstage. I asked Ismael how he knew about Grandma's song. He explained that the song was about coming to a new country and having to leave those you love behind. People put their hands over their hearts to show that their hearts remain in Puerto Rico even though they may be far away. Now I understood why Grandma's song was special to so many people.

Over the next days and weeks, Grandma and I put on our own shows imitating Cortijo's band. Grandma wished such a special night had been captured in a recording so that she could listen to it again and again. But even then I knew that a concert is so special because it leaves you with the memory of a magical moment in time.

As I got older, I started bringing over my records to play for Grandma — Brazilian music, jazz, and even rap. She loved listening to it all.

Even now, when I'm playing CDs in my studio, I imagine I'm back in Grandma's living room and she turns to me and says, "You be the DJ today. *Siempre me gusta tu selección.*" And as I work, Grandma's special song surrounds me.

Think About the Selection

1. What is so special about Grandma's favorite song?

2. The boy and his grandmother listen to music on records and at a live concert. Compare these experiences. Use details from the story.

3. What are some things that the boy learns from his grandmother? How do these compare with things that you've learned from your family?

4. Look at the illustration on page 196. Why do you think this illustration is different from the others?

5. What does the author mean when he says "Grandma wrapped me in her world of music"?

6. **Connecting/Comparing** Both this story and *The Keeping Quilt* tell about sharing traditions. How are these traditions the same and different?

Comparing/Contrasting

Write a Comparison

Make a list of the boy's hobbies and interests. Then make a list of your own hobbies and interests. In a paragraph, explain how your interests and the boy's are different and how they are the same.

Tips

- Reread the parts of the story that describe what the boy likes.
- Make a Venn diagram to sort the activities.

Art

Draw an Album Cover

The boy in *Grandma's Records* likes to draw album covers. Think about your favorite band. Create an album cover for that band. Include the band's name and a title for the album.

Listening/Speaking

Introduce the Band

At a concert, the lead singer will often introduce the band members. With a partner, take turns role-playing what the singer in *Grandma's Records* might say about the other band members. Make sure to mention what instrument each band member plays.

Tips

- Begin with "Ladies and gentlemen. . . ."
- Use expression to get the audience's attention.

Internet

Complete a Word Web Find

Pick up a pencil and record some words you've learned in the story. Print a word-find puzzle from Education Place.

www.eduplace.com/kids

Talented Kids

Music Maestro
Baylen Brooks, 15

by Judith E. Rinard

"I love the sound of a choir, the pureness and beauty of the voices blending," says Baylen Brooks of Front Royal, Virginia. Baylen is one of the youngest people ever to direct a choir. At age eleven he founded the Voices of Salvation Community Choir, a group of about twenty-five adults that he directs. Baylen also sings and accompanies the choir on piano. The choir performs a wide range of music, including soul and gospel tunes and hymns.

"I grew up with gospel music," says Baylen, who started singing in a church choir with his parents when he was two years old. Several years after that choir broke up, he started his own. "At first I was nervous conducting adults," he says. "But now we're like one big family."

Keyed Up
Thristan Mendoza, 12

by Janet Bouy

Thristan may enjoy picking out "Looney Tunes" melodies on his xylophone-like marimba, but when he played for two Filipino presidents, it was serious music all the way. Despite a developmental disorder, the award-winning musician never stops wowing audiences.

Photographic Memory

Thristan has autism, a disorder that affects his social and language skills. But he also has the ability to easily memorize almost any song. "My favorite pieces are classical — they're the most challenging," he says. "But I also like music from shows like *The Powerpuff Girls*."

Keeping the Beat

In addition to performing, Thristan is also recording a marimba album. (The proceeds will help others with autism.) And though the honor student enjoys video games, he's serious about the marimba — most of the time. "I want to inspire people with my music," Thristan says. "But sometimes I'll play silly songs just to make my little brother laugh!"

→

211

Young Mariachi Music Makers

by Ann Jordan

Iris Vidaurri, 11

April Gonzales, 11

April Gonzalez and Iris Vidaurri play with a mariachi band in San Antonio, Texas. Mariachi groups originated in Mexico as strolling musicians. The lively blend of violins, guitars, and trumpets has become a popular music style in the United States.

Iris and April are following in the footsteps of relatives who also play in a band. Iris has been a mariachi for more than six years. Beginning as a guitarist, she switched to the violin after four years. April, with three-and-a-half years' experience, also studied guitar before becoming a violinist. She explains, "The violin is harder, but I think it is fun!"

The eleven year-olds practice forty-five minutes a day. They rehearse with their band, *Sonidos De Alegria* (Sounds of Joy), once a week. They enjoy performing at the outdoor Arneson River Theater, where the San Antonio River flows between the stage and the audience.

Sounds Great!
Jamie Lynn Bence, 10

by Jerry Dunn

"Oh-h! Say, can you see. . . ." That's Jamie Lynn Bence belting out "The Star Spangled Banner" in yet another baseball park. She became the first person to sing America's national anthem in all thirty major league baseball stadiums.

Jamie Lynn actually enjoys singing all alone before 50,000 people. "I just love big crowds!" says the fifth-grader from Hartland, Wisconsin.

The national anthem affects people emotionally, she says. "It seems like you can stop the whole stadium for a second. It's neat." Another fun part of her singing tour is sampling ballpark hot dogs. "Kansas City's are the biggest," she says.

Jamie Lynn began singing at age five and practices up to two hours every day. When she sings, she really concentrates. "If I didn't, I might miss a note, or my voice would crack," she explains.

Background and Vocabulary

The Talking Cloth

THE TALKING CLOTH

STORY AND PICTURES BY Rhonda Mitchell

Read to find the meanings of these words.

e • Glossary

collection
embroidered
royalty
symbols
wealth

Handmade Cloth from Ghana

The Ashanti are a group of people from Ghana, a country in West Africa. The Ashanti make a beautiful kind of cloth called adinkra cloth. In the past, adinkra cloth was very expensive. Having an adinkra cloth was a sign of **wealth**. **Royalty**, such as kings and queens, often wore it. But today, the markets of Ghana are filled with adinkra cloth.

Adinkra cloth is a beautiful ▶ **way to remember the past, and the Ashanti people are proud to wear it.**

One store in a market might have a **collection** of many different cloths.

Parts of the adinkra cloth have colorful, **embroidered** patterns. Other parts are stamped with **symbols**. Each symbol has a different meaning. In the next story, you will learn how these symbols often tell something about the person who wears the cloth.

Europe

Asia

Africa

Ghana

Atlantic Ocean

215

Meet the
AUTHOR AND ILLUSTRATOR

Rhonda Mitchell

Birthday: February 22

Where she was born: Cleveland, Ohio

How she became a children's book illustrator:
Mitchell has always enjoyed painting pictures of people.
One day, a children's author named Angela Johnson
asked Mitchell to paint pictures for some of her books.
Mitchell did, and she loved it!

Why "The Talking Cloth" is important to her:
Mitchell liked illustrating children's books so much that
she decided to write one of her own. *The Talking Cloth*
is the first book she has written. And, of course, she
also painted the pictures.

Some other things she likes:
Cats, tennis, living in a small town

Find out more about Rhonda Mitchell by visiting
Education Place. **www.eduplace.com/kids**

Selection 3

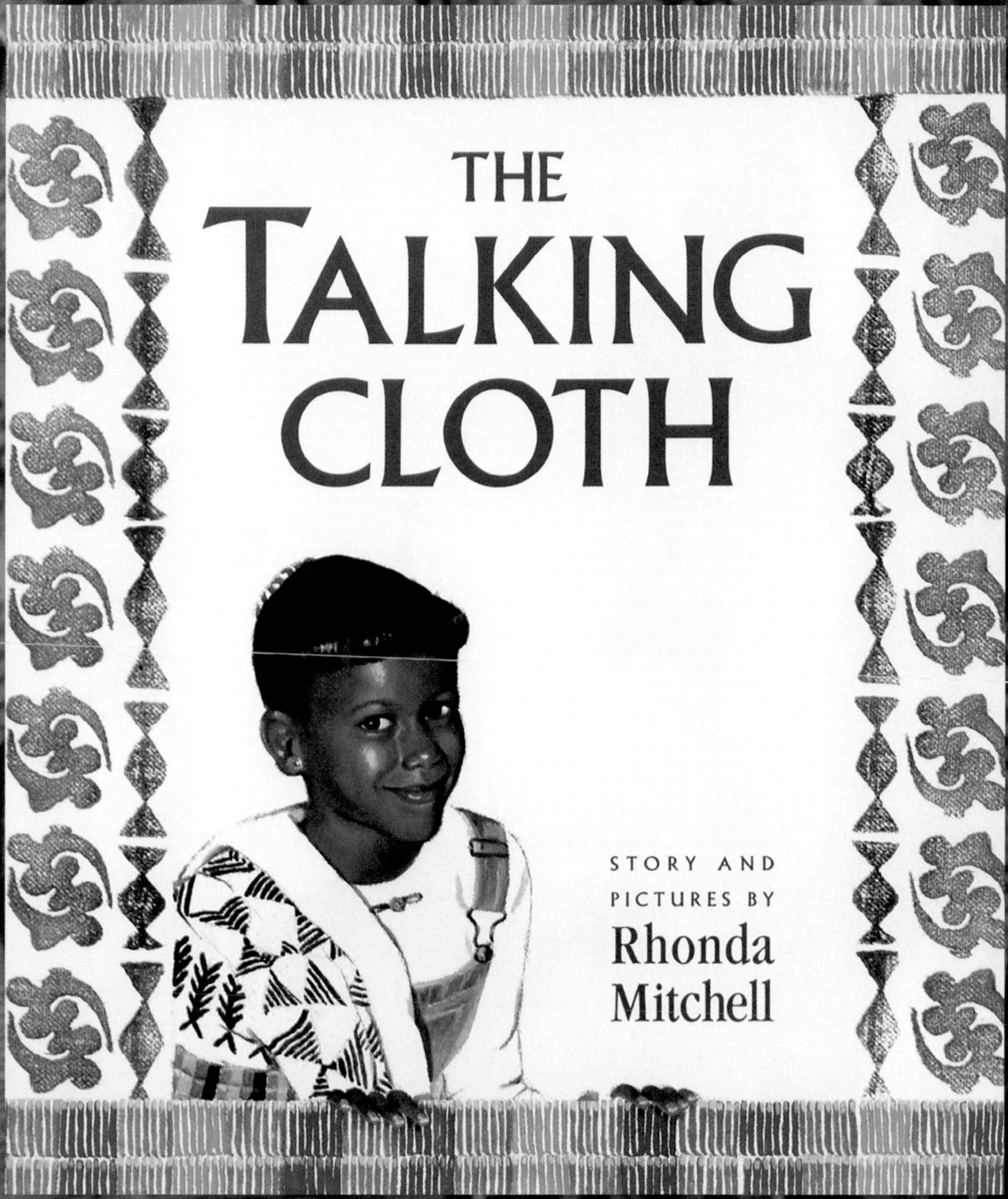
THE TALKING CLOTH
STORY AND PICTURES BY
Rhonda Mitchell

Strategy Focus

As you read, **summarize** what the Talking Cloth means to Amber and her family.

Aunt Phoebe has things. Things and things and things.

"A collector of life," Mom calls her.

Daddy says she lives in a junk pile.

"Reminds me of your room, Amber," he says.

I like visiting Aunt Phoebe. There's no place in
her house to be bored, and she always gives me mocha
to drink. Daddy says it will stunt my growth.

Aunt Phoebe tells him, "Mocha is named after a
city in Yemen, and this child just grew an inch or two,
inside, for knowing that."

Aunt Phoebe knows things. . . .

She tells me stories, about her "collection of life,"
each time we visit. I sip hot mocha and listen, imagining
all the people and places she has seen.

Today we sit in her kitchen and
she tells about the basket of folded
cloths in the corner. "I bought these
in Africa," she says.

Daddy laughs. "I figured that
was laundry you hadn't put away."

Aunt Phoebe smiles and takes a cloth from the top of the basket. She unfolds it with a flourish — a long magic carpet. It runs like a white river across the floor.

"What do you do with such a long cloth?" I ask.

"You wear it," says Aunt Phoebe. "It tells how you are feeling. This cloth talks."

"How can it do that?"

"By its color and what the symbols mean," Aunt Phoebe tells me. "This is *adinkra* cloth from Ghana. It's made by the Ashanti people and at one time only royalty wore it," she says.

Aunt Phoebe rubs the cloth against my face. It's silk and feels smooth. I imagine myself an Ashanti princess. . . .

The cloth is embroidered in sections and hand printed all over with small black symbols. Like words.

A white cloth means joy — yellow, gold or riches. Green stands for newness and growth. Blue is a sign of love, but red is worn only for sad times, like funerals or during wars.

"Maybe I should wear red when your daddy comes to visit," Aunt Phoebe says.

Daddy laughs and pours himself some mocha. He likes to listen too. I know it.

Aunt Phoebe tells the meaning of some symbols on her cloth. One says, "Except God I fear none." That's called *Gye Nyame*.

Another is called *Obi nka Obie*. "I offend no one without cause."

Each symbol speaks of something different, like faith, power, or love.

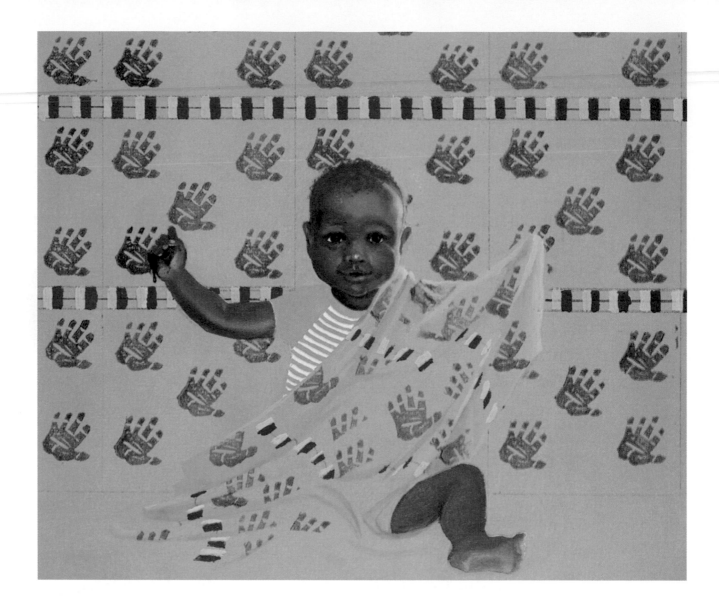

I imagine cloths with my own symbols on them.

Fred — he's my little brother — should be dressed in green for "go" with grubby little handprints all over. Everyone can see what kind of a mess that kid is.

Aunt Phoebe's little brother is my daddy. "Let's see," she says. "Guess we could wrap him in gray pinstripe cloth for seriousness, with squares on it!"

We all laugh, imagining that.

I ask if I can put on the *adinkra* cloth.

"Of course you can, baby," Aunt Phoebe says. "When you're older, you can have it for your own."

She wraps the *adinkra* three times around my waist, then across one shoulder — and still it drags on the ground.

"A cloth this long is a sign of wealth," she tells me.

Daddy says, "Amber, you'll need to drink a lot of mocha to grow tall enough."

"Well," says Aunt Phoebe, "this child has grown a lot, *inside*, just today!"

I smile, thinking of it. This cloth means joy.
I am an Ashanti princess now, and here is all my family
and everyone who has ever worn an *adinkra* . . .

gathered around me.

Think About the Selection

1. Why do you think Aunt Phoebe likes to collect things?

2. Why does Amber enjoy visiting Aunt Phoebe? Would you like to visit Aunt Phoebe? Explain your answer.

3. How does the Talking Cloth "talk," and what does the cloth say?

4. What does Aunt Phoebe mean when she says that Amber has grown *inside*?

5. If you had an adinkra cloth, what would it look like? What would your cloth say about you?

6. **Connecting/Comparing** How is the Keeping Quilt also a kind of Talking Cloth?

Describing

Write a Character Sketch

Describe your favorite character in the story. Use facts from the story to help you guess the character's favorite activities, items, foods, and clothes. Include adjectives such as *serious* or *adventurous* to describe how the character acts.

Tips

- To get started, create a word web about the character.
- Put the most important details at the beginning of your sketch.

Math

Write Number Sentences

Look carefully at pages 222–223. How many squares do you see in the Talking Cloth? Write number sentences to describe the total number of squares. Try to write at least four different sentences.

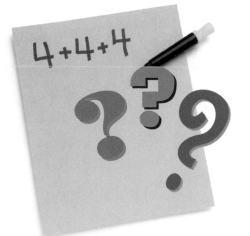

Viewing

Make Symbol Flashcards

Find five symbols in your classroom, neighborhood, or home. Draw each symbol on a different card. On the back of each card, write what the symbol means. Then ask a classmate to guess the meaning of each symbol.

Bonus Create a symbol that says something about you. Ask your partner to guess what it means.

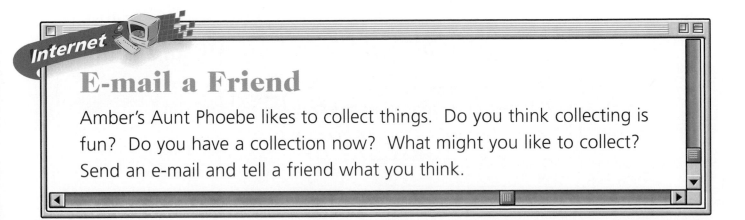

Internet

E-mail a Friend

Amber's Aunt Phoebe likes to collect things. Do you think collecting is fun? Do you have a collection now? What might you like to collect? Send an e-mail and tell a friend what you think.

A Healthy Recipe from Ghana

by Deanna F. Cook

Skill: How to Follow a Recipe

❶ **Find** a grown-up to watch you in case you need help.

❷ **Read** the recipe carefully.

❸ **Gather** all the ingredients and kitchen tools you'll need.

❹ **Reread** each step before you follow it.

❺ **Follow** the steps in the correct order.

In Ghana, peanuts are called groundnuts because they grow underground. Ghanians eat groundnuts — a big source of protein — almost every day. To make peanut butter, they mash groundnuts using a mortar and pestle. If you have a food processor, this is a faster way to make it.

Homemade Peanut Butter

2 cups (500 ml) unsalted roasted peanuts

1 tablespoon (15 ml) vegetable oil

Here's What You Do

1 Pour the shelled peanuts and vegetable oil into the bowl of a food processor.

2 With the help of a grown-up, process the peanuts for about 3 minutes, or until smooth.

Makes 1 cup (250 ml) of all-natural, creamy peanut butter. Put any leftovers in the refrigerator.

Dancing Rainbows

Evelyn Clarke Mott

Read to find
the meanings
of these words.

e ● Glossary

ancestors

elders

honor

imitating

respect

NATIVE AMERICAN DANCE

Dance has always been an important part of many Native American cultures. Native American children often learn to dance by **imitating** older members of their family or community. The **elders** may teach children different traditional dances that have been performed for a long time.

These dances can have many meanings. In some dances, Native Americans show **respect** for their **ancestors** who have lived before them. In others, they **honor** the sun and the earth.

Through their traditional dances, Native Americans remember their past and share their memories and history with each other. Dancing is one way they celebrate their lives.

This Native American dancer wears a traditional costume as she performs.

234

Young Native Americans, such as the boy in the next selection, may enjoy performing and watching traditional dances.

Meet the
Author and Photographer
Evelyn Clarke Mott

Fact File

▶ Mott was born on August 22 in Portchester, New York.

▶ At the age of ten, Mott won three dollars in a newspaper's writing contest.

▶ For her book *Balloon Ride*, Mott had to ride in a hot-air balloon. There was only one problem — she was afraid of high places! At first, it was hard to take pictures because her hands and legs were shaking. After a while, she lost her fear and finished the book.

▶ Mott also likes music, art, hiking, traveling, and looking at the stars.

Internet

You can learn more about Evelyn Clarke Mott by visiting Education Place. **www.eduplace.com/kids**

DANCING RAINBOWS

A Pueblo Boy's Story

Evelyn Clarke Mott

How are dancing, rain, and rainbows important to Curt and his family? As you read, **monitor** your understanding. Reread to **clarify** anything that's confusing.

237

It is the day before Feast Day. Curt and his grandpa, Andy, are excited. Every year, on June 24, their pueblo has a big party with food, fun, and dance.

Pueblo is a Spanish word for town. Curt and Andy Garcia are Pueblo Indians. Their tribe is called Tewa. They live in San Juan Pueblo, New Mexico.

San Juan Pueblo is named after Saint John. On Feast Day, native dances honor the pueblo's patron saint and celebrate the power of the summer sun.

Curt's ancestors were farmers. They grew corn, beans, and squash. Now most Tewas work at businesses outside the pueblo, but some still farm.

"We must always take care of our land," Andy tells Curt. "We must respect Mother Earth."

Curt spends a lot of time with his grandpa. He learns so much. They share many laughs.

Andy is an elder in his tribe. That means he is very respected. He is well known among his people as a great dancer. "Dance with all your heart!" Andy says.

All Tewa dances are prayers. The Tewa people dance to cure the sick, to give thanks, to bring the tribe together, to pray for good crops, and to have fun! Because the Tewas' land is very dry, every dance is also a prayer for rain.

"Let's hurry, Grandpa!" Curt says. "It's time for the Buffalo Dance!" Curt and Andy rush to the plaza.

The plaza is the center of town. It is where the tribe meets. Three people dance in buffalo costume.

Tewas believe that people and animals once spoke the same language. This ended when people started to lose respect for the animals. Tewas show their respect for all animals with the Buffalo Dance. This dance blesses tomorrow's Feast Day. It is said to give the tribe strength and power.

The smell of baking bread welcomes Curt and Andy home from the dance. For Feast Day, Curt's mom and relatives all help bake over seventy loaves of bread in the horno, an oven for baking bread, cakes, and cookies. It is shaped like a beehive.

The horno sits outside the house. Curt's mom makes a fire to heat up the oven. Then she cleans out the ashes and puts in the dough.

The dough bakes in the warm oven. Curt's mom pulls out the hot bread. Dogs wait near the horno eager for a taste!

The Garcia house smells of stew, bread, cakes, and candy. Everyone looks forward to tomorrow's feast!

Andy wakes up early on Feast Day. He prays in the hills. He asks for a good mind, a good heart, and a good life. He sprinkles some cornmeal as a gift to the earth.

Today looks bright and sunny. But even if it rains, everyone will dance. Tewas believe rain is good luck. They say their ancestors come back as raindrops to help them live.

Rainbows are also good luck. They join Mother Earth with Father Sky.

Soon all the Garcias are awake. Everyone hurries to get ready. Andy's wife, Verna, sprinkles salt on his head. She says it keeps away bad spirits.

Andy helps Curt put on face paint. Curt pulls a fox skin over his head. He puts on his Comanche costume.

Andy fixes his bustle. He ties on his headdress. With everyone ready, the Garcias head toward the plaza.

BOOM! BOOM! BOOM! The drummers move through the crowd.

Indians say drums have great power. They believe a drum sounds the heartbeat of Mother Earth. Drummers paint their hands white to give their drumbeats more power.

The drummers sing in Tewa. They sing of many things. Plants. Animals. Clouds. Rainbows. They try to sing like birds. Bird songs are so beautiful.

The Comanche Dance starts. Over a hundred Tewas, from three to eighty years old, move their feet to the beat of the drum.

In this dance, they are imitating the Comanche warriors, acting as they would in battle. The dancers pray for the Tewa tribe and give thanks for their blessings.

Colors twirl and swirl.

Andy dances proudly.

Tewas dance their thanks to the Great Spirit. They pray for their tribe's happiness. They pray for Mother Earth.

Jingle . . . Jingle . . . Jingle. Bells ring as Curt moves his feet. He thinks of his grandpa's words, "A Tewa never dances for himself. He dances for all things and people." Curt sends out prayers to the crowd. He wishes them a good life and a safe trip home.

In 1923, the United States made Indian worship illegal. Tewas could no longer visit their kivas — a place of worship. Indians could not dance. All Indian dances were seen as war dances. It wasn't until 1934 that Indians could dance again.

Now, at Feast Day, the flag flies proudly. Many Tewas have fought for their country. Some dancers show pride for their country.

Tewa women dance with grace. To celebrate the power of the sun, they paint the red sun on their cheeks.

The men yelp loudly for the Comanche Dance. They wear fancy costumes.

Tewa children dance with honor. They learn to dance as soon as they walk. That is why they are good, strong dancers.

Costumes have many meanings. Shells sound like waves hitting the shore. Tassels look like raindrops. Bells sound like falling rain. Embroidered designs look like clouds.

The dancers go home for the feast. Tewa homes fill with friends and family. There is so much to eat. Andy says he doesn't hear any talking. Only chewing!

After the feast, everyone meets at the plaza. They dance again in the hot sun. As the sun sets, the dancers go home.

Sometimes, Curt and Andy practice their dances. Andy teaches Curt. Curt respects his grandpa because he is very wise. Curt tries to be like his grandpa.

Curt and his brothers do the Eagle Dance. They swoop, soar, land, circle, and rest. They keep perfect time to the beat of the drum.

The eagle flies <u>higher than</u> any other bird. Tewas believe that eagles are messengers. They say that eagles bring prayers to the clouds and messages back to the earth. Tewas dance to give thanks to the great bird.

Andy started a dance group for Curt and other young
Tewa dancers. The group often dances outside the pueblo.
Fairs. Schools. Hospitals. Powwows.

The day after Feast Day, Curt dances at a city fair.
He says it doesn't matter where he dances. His prayers
still reach the clouds.

Curt is proud to be Tewa. His ancestors have given him so much. Beautiful songs. Colorful dances. Curt is happy to follow his grandpa's footsteps. Dancing for rain. And rainbows.

Think About the Selection

1. Why do you think Curt respects his grandpa and tries to be like him?

2. Why does Andy start a dance group for young Tewas?

3. How does Curt follow Andy's advice to "dance with all your heart"? What do *you* do with all your heart?

4. What does Andy mean when he says, "A Tewa never dances for himself. He dances for all things and people"?

5. How does Andy teach younger family members about the past? What are some ways *you* learn about the past?

6. **Connecting/Comparing** Compare the tradition shared by Curt and his grandpa with the one shared by the boy and his grandmother in *Grandma's Records*. How are they alike and different?

Explaining

Write an Explanation

How do Curt and his family prepare for the Feast Day? Write an explanation that tells what each person does to get ready for the celebration.

Tips

- To begin, go back to the selection and take notes.
- Organize your explanation by topic, main ideas, and supporting details.

Social Studies

Link Geography to Your Community

In a small group, look at the big photograph on pages 244–245. Describe the land and climate where Curt and Andy live. Discuss how their surroundings affect life in their community. Then discuss how your surroundings affect life in your own community.

Science

Draw the Water Cycle

Where does rain come from, and where does it go? Draw a diagram explaining the water cycle. Include the earth, water, sun, air, clouds, and rain. Use arrows to show the path of the water. Label each part of the cycle. Use an encyclopedia or a science book for information.

Bonus Show how the water cycle changes at different times of the year.

Internet

Send an E-postcard

Choose one of the traditions you have discovered in this theme so far. Send a friend an E-postcard telling him or her all about it. You'll find one at Education Place. **www.eduplace.com/kids**

Rain and Rainbows

by Neil Ardley

Why does a dazzling arch of color form when the sun lights up a rain shower? Find out by adding a little sunshine to a bowl of water.

Did You Know?

You can see a rainbow in a rain shower if the sun is behind you. Each raindrop is a round mass of water that splits the sunlight into different colors and reflects them back at you.

Making a Rainbow

Fishbowl filled with water   **Black cardboard**   **White cardboard**

1. Move a table to a sunny place. Lay the black cardboard on the table, then set the fishbowl on top.

2. Hold the white cardboard off to one side of the fishbowl. Hold it so that the side of the cardboard facing you is shaded. A rainbow appears on the cardboard!

As the sunlight passes through the round mass of water, it splits into the colors of the rainbow, which are reflected onto the cardboard.

259

Check Your Progress

In this theme, you have learned about different family traditions. Here's a chance to read about two more traditions and compare them with the others. You will also practice your test-taking skills.

In her letter, Patricia Polacco says that traditions are passed down from older family members. How do the selections in this theme fit with this idea?

Now it's time to read about how two more families celebrate their traditions. As you read, think about what makes each tradition special.

Read and Compare

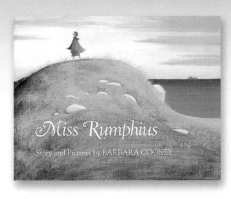

Miss Rumphius has one important thing left on her to-do list.

Try these strategies:
Evaluate
Predict and Infer

Ryan's family prepares for the Chinese New Year.

Try these strategies:
Summarize
Question

Strategies in Action *Look for ways to use all your reading strategies while you read.*

Miss Rumphius

written and illustrated by Barbara Cooney

When Alice Rumphius was young, she told her grandfather that she would do two things. She would visit faraway places when she grew up, and she would live by the sea when she became old. But her grandfather told her that there was a third thing she needed to do. Now Miss Rumphius is an adult. She has seen the world and has settled in a home by the sea. But there is still one more thing she has to do.

From the porch of her new house Miss Rumphius watched the sun come up; she watched it cross the heavens and sparkle on the water; and she saw it set in glory in the evening. She started a little garden among the rocks that surrounded her house, and she planted a few flower seeds in the stony ground. Miss Rumphius was *almost* perfectly happy.

"But there is still one more thing I have to do," she said. "I have to do something to make the world more beautiful."

But what? "The world already is pretty nice," she thought, looking out over the ocean.

The next spring Miss Rumphius was not very
well. Her back was bothering her again, and she had
to stay in bed most of the time.

The flowers she had planted the summer before
had come up and bloomed in spite of the stony
ground. She could see them from her bedroom
window, blue and purple and rose-colored.

"Lupines," said Miss Rumphius with satisfaction.
"I have always loved lupines the best. I wish I could
plant more seeds this summer so that I could have
still more flowers next year."

But she was not able to.

After a hard winter spring came. Miss Rumphius
was feeling much better. Now she could take walks
again. One afternoon she started to go up and over
the hill, where she had not been in a long time.

"I don't believe my eyes!" she cried when she got
to the top. For there on the other side of the hill
was a large patch of blue and purple and rose-colored
lupines!

"It was the wind," she said as she knelt in
delight. "It was the wind that brought the seeds
from my garden here! And the birds must have
helped!"

Then Miss Rumphius had a wonderful idea!

She hurried home and got out her seed catalogues. She sent off to the very best seed house for five bushels of lupine seed.

All that summer Miss Rumphius, her pockets full of seeds, wandered over fields and headlands, sowing lupines. She scattered seeds along the highways and down the country lanes. She flung handfuls of them around the schoolhouse and back of the church. She tossed them into hollows and along stone walls.

Her back didn't hurt her any more at all. . . .

The next spring there were lupines everywhere.
Fields and hillsides were covered with blue and purple
and rose-colored flowers. They bloomed along the
highways and down the lanes. Bright patches lay around

the schoolhouse and back of the church. Down in the hollows and along the stone walls grew the beautiful flowers.

Miss Rumphius had done the third, the most difficult thing of all!

My Great-aunt Alice, Miss Rumphius, is very old now. Her hair is very white. Every year there are more and more lupines. Now they call her the Lupine Lady. Sometimes my friends stand with me outside her gate, curious to see the old, old lady who planted the fields of lupines. When she invites us in, they come slowly. They think she is the oldest woman in the world. Often she tells us stories of faraway places.

"When I grow up," I tell her, "I too will go to faraway places and come home to live by the sea."

"That is all very well, little Alice," says my aunt, "but there is a third thing you must do."

"What is that?" I ask.

"You must do something to make the world more beautiful."

"All right," I say.

But I do not know yet
what that can be.

Celebrating Chinese New Year

by Dianne Hoyt-Goldsmith
photographs by Lawrence Migdale

In the Chinese culture, Chinese New Year is a
special holiday. The New Year celebration
lasts for fifteen days and ends with a parade.
A boy named Ryan enjoys the holiday with his
family, buying fruit and other foods that are
said to bring good luck.

On the first day of the New Year, family and friends
go visiting. They bring oranges, tangerines, and sweets
as gifts. There is a Chinese tradition that if you haven't

paid a visit to your relatives by the third day of the New Year, it is best not to go at all. That means that you won't get along for the rest of the year.

For Ryan's family, the best part of the Chinese New Year celebration is a big dinner for the entire family. Eating a meal together on New Year's Day shows the importance of family unity. Ryan's family invites all their relatives who live in San Francisco. Ryan's grandmother, aunts, uncles, and cousins will all be there. His parents, as hosts of the meal, plan an elaborate menu.

The New Year's feast takes many days to prepare. There is shopping for all the ingredients and then the careful preparation. Ryan's father, who is a professional chef, enjoys cooking traditional dishes. Ryan always likes to help.

All the food for New Year's Day is prepared before the New Year begins. The Chinese say that if a person works on New Year's Day, he will have to work that much harder all through the coming year.

Ryan's father plans a menu with many special New Year's dishes. He will serve chicken and duck. These will be cut up after cooking, but then put back together on the serving platter, including the heads and feet, to symbolize completeness and family unity. Eating these foods is said to help keep the family together.

Think and Compare

1. Both *Miss Rumphius* and *Chinese New Year* tell about traditions that are passed along. How are these traditions alike? How are they different?

2. How do traditions help younger people and older people feel closer? Use examples from this theme.

3. Both Miss Rumphius and Aunt Phoebe in *The Talking Cloth* share beautiful things with other people. Why do you think they choose to do this?

4. Compare a tradition in this theme with one in your own life. How are the traditions alike or different?

Strategies in Action Tell about two or three places in *Miss Rumphius* where you used reading strategies.

Write an Opinion

Are traditions important to you? Write your opinion telling why or why not. Use details from your own experience or from the selections in the theme.

Tips

- Begin by stating your opinion clearly.
- Think of three reasons to support your opinion.
- Think of details to support each reason.

Filling in the Blank

Some test items ask you to complete a sentence. You must choose the best answer from three or four choices. A test about *Miss Rumphius* might include this sentence.

Read the sentence. Fill in the circle for the answer that best completes the sentence.

1 The "one more thing" that Miss Rumphius says she has to do is _____.

- ○ plant a little garden
- ● make the world more beautiful
- ○ get more exercise
- ○ take walks

 Understand the sentence.

Find the key words in the sentence. Use them to understand what you need to do.

> I think the key words are *one more thing*. I need to find out what Miss Rumphius still needs to do.

② Look back at the selection.

Think about where to find the answer. You may need to look in more than one place. Use the key words to skim the selection.

> I can find this near the beginning, before Miss Rumphius gets sick. It sounds like the answer could set up the story. I'll start there.

③ Narrow the choices. Then choose the best answer.

Try each answer choice in the blank as you read the sentence. Find the choices that are clearly wrong. Have a good reason for choosing an answer. Guess only if you have to.

> The first choice happens too early, and the third choice is not in the story. The fourth choice could be right, but it's not important. The second choice is correct.

TRICKSTER TALES

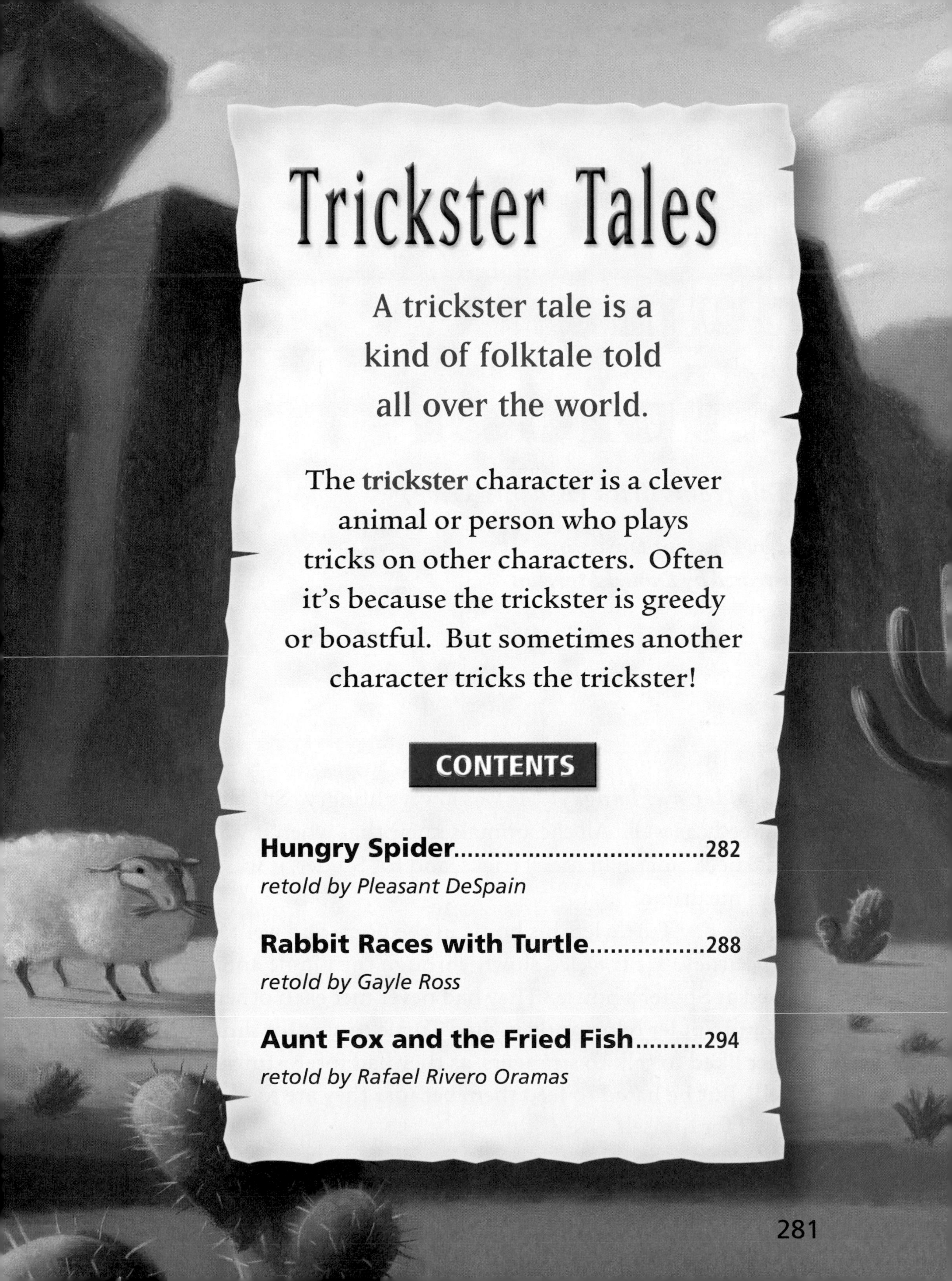

Trickster Tales

A trickster tale is a
kind of folktale told
all over the world.

The **trickster** character is a clever
animal or person who plays
tricks on other characters. Often
it's because the trickster is greedy
or boastful. But sometimes another
character tricks the trickster!

CONTENTS

Focus on Genre

Hungry Spider

A Tale from Africa (Ashanti Tribe)

told by Pleasant DeSpain
illustrated by Daniel Moreton

Spider was hungry! He was always hungry. Spider was greedy as well. All the animals knew that when it was mealtime, Spider had many tricks, and for Spider, it was always mealtime.

One day Turtle left his home in the pond and went on a long journey. He traveled slowly through the jungle and finally arrived at Spider's house. They had never met each other before this, and Spider reluctantly invited Turtle to stay for dinner. Spider liked to talk to strangers, as they had interesting stories to tell. But he hated to feed them because they ate food that he wanted for himself.

"Friend Turtle," said Spider, "you must be tired after your long trip. Go down to the river and refresh yourself. I'll prepare our dinner while you are gone."

"How kind of you," said Turtle. "I'll hurry as I'm quite hungry." Turtle followed the trail to the water's edge and scrambled in. It was good to cool down and feel clean again. He crawled out of the river and hurried back to Spider's house. Delicious odors filled the air. It was time to eat!

Turtle walked in and saw the food on the table. "Thank you for inviting me to stay for dinner, Spider," said Turtle. "I haven't eaten all day."

"You are most welcome, Turtle," said Spider with a frown. "But in this part of the country, we don't sit at the table with muddy feet."

Turtle looked at his feet. Indeed, they were muddy. His feet were wet from the river and the trail was thick with dust. He was most embarrassed. He excused himself and walked all the way back to the river to wash them off. He dried them carefully on the grass and hurried back to Spider. But he was too late. Spider had eaten all the food. Turtle was disappointed, but too polite to complain. He slept hungry that night and left for home in the morning even hungrier!

Several months later, Spider went on a long journey. He arrived at Turtle's house and asked if he could spend the night.

"Of course, friend Spider," said Turtle. "I remember how good you were to me."

"I'm famished!" exclaimed Spider. "Could we eat right away?"

"I'll dive to the bottom of the pond and prepare a feast," said Turtle. "Wait here and I'll call you when all is ready."

Turtle gathered his best-tasting food and set it on a long table at the bottom of the pond. Then he swam to the surface and said, "Please join me, Spider. Dinner is served."

Spider leaped into the water and tried to dive down. But he weighed so little that he couldn't stay underwater, let alone sink to the bottom. Turtle had already started to eat, so Spider kicked and jerked and splashed with all of his strength. And he stayed right on top.

Turtle swam to the surface and said, "Friend Spider, come down and enjoy the meal. It's quite good, if I do say so."

Spider had an idea! He scrambled back to shore and picked up several heavy pebbles. He stuffed them in his coat pockets to weigh him down. Spider then hopped back into the pond and sank quickly to the bottom. The food was half gone, but what was left looked delicious! He had started to take a big bite when Turtle said, "Friend Spider, in this part of the jungle, it's considered bad manners to eat with your coat on."

Spider didn't want to be impolite. So he slipped out of his coat and reached for another morsel of food. But before he could grab hold of it, he bobbed to the surface like a cork! Spider cried as he floated about, watching Turtle down on the bottom of the pond eating the rest of the food.

It is said that one kindness deserves another.

Rabbit Races with Turtle

told by Gayle Ross
illustrated by Murv Jacob

It is true that Rabbit loved to brag and exaggerate about all the things he could do, but one thing that everyone agreed on was that he was a very fast runner. Turtle loved to boast too, however, and one day he told the people that he was even faster than Rabbit. Rabbit heard about Turtle's claim, and they

began to argue so fiercely that everyone agreed the only way to settle the matter was to have a race between the two. It was decided that Turtle and Rabbit would race over four mountain ridges, and the one who came over the fourth ridge first would be the winner.

Now, no one had ever seen Turtle move at anything but the slowest of paces, so Rabbit was certain of his ability to win. So sure was he that he told Turtle, "You know you can't run. You could never win a race with me. I will give you the first ridge. You will have to cross only three, while I cross all four."

Turtle agreed to Rabbit's terms, but that night he called together all his turtle relatives. "You must help me put an end to Rabbit's boasting," said Turtle. He explained his plan to his family, and they all agreed to help.

When the day of the race came, all the animals gathered. Some came to the starting point to see the runners off. Others waited on the fourth ridge to declare the winner. Rabbit came to the starting point, but Turtle had gone ahead to the next ridge as Rabbit had arranged. The others could just see his shiny back through the long grass. The signal was given, and the race began!

Rabbit burst from the starting point with his long jumps, expecting to win the race before Turtle could even make it down his first ridge. Imagine his surprise when he came to the top of the ridge and saw Turtle disappearing over the top of the next mountain!

Rabbit ran even faster, and when he came to the top of the second mountain, he looked all around, expecting to see Turtle somewhere in the long grass. He looked up — and there was the sun glinting off Turtle's shell as he crossed the third ridge!

291

Now Rabbit was truly surprised, and he was beginning to be worried. He gave his longest jumps ever to catch up. When he reached the top of the third ridge, he was so tired and out of breath he could only fall over and cry as he watched Turtle cross the fourth mountain and win the race!

The other animals gave the race to Turtle, and everyone wondered how slow Turtle had managed to beat Rabbit. Turtle just smiled and never spoke of it, but it was really very easy.

All Turtle's relatives look just alike, so Turtle had placed one near the top of each ridge. Whenever Rabbit had come into sight, a Turtle relative had crawled to the top of the mountain ahead of him and then hidden in the tall grass. Turtle himself had climbed the fourth ridge to cross the finish line.

So Turtle won the race with a very good trick of his own. But if he had hoped to stop Rabbit's bragging, he was surely disappointed. No one has ever been able to do that.

Aunt Fox and the Fried Fish

told by Rafael Rivero Oramas
illustrated by Richard Bernal

Early one morning, Uncle Fox was strolling through the forest when he came upon a river full of fish. Watching the fish jump and splash made Uncle Fox very hungry, so he decided to try his luck at fishing. He soon caught three big, beautiful fish.

Uncle Fox rushed home with his catch. "Aunt Fox, come and see what luck I've had today!" he called to his wife.

"Oh my! What huge fish!" cried Aunt Fox, licking her chops hungrily.

"You're right," said Uncle Fox. "You and I won't be able to eat all three of them. Why don't we invite Uncle Tiger to lunch? That would make him happy."

"Excellent, Uncle Fox," agreed Aunt Fox. "Go and invite Uncle Tiger. I'll fry the fish, and we'll have a wonderful meal!" Uncle Fox smiled and went off to find Uncle Tiger.

Aunt Fox put all three fish in a frying pan and placed them on the stove. The mouthwatering smell of fried fish floated through the house.

Aunt Fox's stomach began to grumble and growl. "I should try a piece of my fish," she thought to herself. "What if I didn't use enough salt? But I'll only eat a small piece. After all, it would be terrible if I ate up all my fish before Uncle Fox comes back."

Aunt Fox began nibbling at her fish. How tender and delicious it tasted! She forgot all about waiting for Uncle Fox and Uncle Tiger. In a few seconds, she had licked her plate clean.

"That was tasty!" Aunt Fox exclaimed. "Maybe I should try Uncle Fox's fish. He's very picky. If his fish isn't delightfully crispy and well-seasoned, I'm sure he'll be upset."

So Aunt Fox started nibbling at the second fish. First she ate the tail, then a fin, then the head. Before she knew it, Uncle Fox's fish was gone! "My goodness, I've eaten the whole thing!" Aunt Fox cried.

Now there was only one fish left. "Oh, well," murmured Aunt Fox. "The damage is done. I might as well eat the last one too."

And Aunt Fox gobbled up the third fish.

At last Uncle Fox arrived with Uncle Tiger. "Have you fried the fish?" Uncle Fox asked his wife.

"Of course I have!" she told him. "I put them by the fire so they wouldn't get cold."

"Well, serve them right away. We're starving. Right, Uncle Tiger?"

"Yes, Uncle Fox," agreed Uncle Tiger. "The fish smell so wonderful I can hardly wait to eat."

"Please sit here, Uncle Tiger," said Aunt Fox. "I will set the table."

"Thank you, Aunt Fox," said Uncle Tiger as he sat down.

Before Uncle Fox could sit down, Aunt Fox called him aside. "The fish were old and tough," she whispered. "They will be hard to cut. Go out to the patio and sharpen the knives."

Uncle Fox hurried outside. Soon Aunt Fox and Uncle Tiger could hear the harsh sound of Uncle Fox scraping knives against a stone.

Aunt Fox rushed over to Uncle Tiger. "Do you hear that?" she cried. "That's my husband, sharpening a knife. He's gone crazy! He told me he wants to eat your ears, Uncle Tiger! That's why he invited you for lunch. Run — before he comes back inside!"

Terrified, Uncle Tiger raced out of the house. Just then, Aunt Fox shouted, "Uncle Fox! Uncle Fox! Come quickly! Uncle Tiger has stolen all our fish!"

Uncle Fox dashed after Uncle Tiger. "Uncle Tiger, Uncle Tiger, please come back!" he begged. "Let me have at least one of them!"

Uncle Tiger, who thought Uncle Fox was begging for his ears, fled in fear. Faster and faster he ran. And he didn't stop until he reached his home, safe and sound.

Think About the
TRICKSTER TALES

1. Compare the tricks played by the characters. Which do you think is the most clever? Which one is funniest? Why?

2. Do you think the characters had good reasons or bad reasons for playing tricks? Explain.

3. How could the tricksters have solved their problems without playing a trick?

4. Who was your favorite trickster character? Why?

Internet

Take an Online Quiz

What do you know about trickster tales? Here's a chance to test what you have learned by taking our online quiz.

www.eduplace.com/kids

Creating

Write Your Own Trickster Tale

Choose an animal trickster. Use
one you've just read about, or choose
another popular trickster, such as a wolf or a coyote.
What will your trickster be like — greedy, boastful,
clever, rude? Decide what other animals your tale
will include. Who will be tricked in this battle of
wits, your trickster or the other characters?

Tips

- Use a story map to organize the elements of your tale.
- Introduce the characters, the setting, and the problem in a few sentences.
- Keep the events of the plot quick and simple.
- Write lots of lively dialogue.

301

Incredible Stories

Read . . . Think . . . Dream

Ride me the waves
    of a story,
Settle me down
    by a brook,
Dream me a land
    only dreamed of,
Book me a voyage
    by book.

J. Patrick Lewis

Incredible Stories

with Jerdine Nolen

Dear Friends,

Welcome to *Incredible Stories*! What makes a story incredible? Where do ideas for incredible stories come from?

Ideas for my incredible stories often come up when I least expect them to. Ideas come to me when I'm laughing out loud, sitting very quietly, or doing fun and exciting chores, like washing the dishes.

That is how I got the idea for *Raising Dragons*. I was standing at the kitchen sink, listening to my two young children playing at my feet. I glanced out the kitchen window and thought, "There are enough dishes in this sink to hold the amount of food a baby dragon eats in one day!" I laughed as the first sentence of *Raising Dragons* came to me. I put those pots and pans away fast and ran to my writing desk.

Sometimes I get ideas for incredible stories from my idea box. I look inside the idea box and just like that, something that can lead to an incredible story POPS right out at me.

Look at the sombrero in my idea box. It could be a hat worn by a Great Dane named. . .how about Muscles? Or is the sombrero a smaller mountain sitting next to a larger mountain?

Is the piece of blue ribbon a rolling river? Or is the ribbon part of the sky that floated to the ground the day Muscles got lost? Did Muscles find a quarter? Or is the quarter a person trapped inside a mirror who needs Muscles' help to escape?

As you can see, everyday things can lead to incredible stories. After reading the following selections, you may never look at *anything* the same way again.

Your friend,

Jardine Nolen

Stories Come to Life!

Think about where Jerdine Nolen gets her story ideas. Look around you. What do you see that could be an idea for an incredible story?

As you read each selection in this theme, think about what makes it incredible and what parts could really happen.

Don't worry about choosing a favorite story in this theme. They're all incredible stories!

DINOSAUR BOB
AND HIS ADVENTURES WITH THE FAMILY LAZARDO
by William Joyce

Fugitives on
Four Legs
NATIONAL GEOGRAPHIC
World
WHITE
by Jean Kaplan Teichroew

DOGZILLA

THE MYSTERIOUS
GIANT OF BARLETTA
An Italian folktale adapted and illustrated by
TOMIE DePAOLA

Raising
Dragons
WRITTEN BY
Jerdine Nolen
ILLUSTRATED BY
Elise Primavera

THE GARDEN OF ABDUL GASAZI
Written and Illustrated by CHRIS VAN ALLSBURG

Internet To learn about the authors in this theme, visit Education Place. **www.eduplace.com/kids**

Background and Vocabulary

Dogzilla

Written and directed by
DAV PILKEY

Read to find the meanings of these words.

e ● Glossary

colossal

creature

heroic

horrifying

monstrous

terrifying

tremendous

MOVIE MONSTERS

Look out! Watching a huge **creature** destroy everything in its path can be **terrifying**, even if it's only make-believe. That's what makes movie monsters both **horrifying** and fun to watch.

A movie monster uses its **tremendous** strength and size to scare everyone. To defeat a monster, people must be smart and brave. They must do **heroic** things to save themselves, their town, and maybe even the world. They can do it, though. And it's all just good, scary fun.

A movie monster surprises these boys in 1954.

The story you are about to read is based on a famous movie monster named Godzilla. Godzilla is a colossal, 300-foot-tall, fire-breathing lizard.

It's Alive! **GODZILLA** KING OF THE MONSTERS!

RAYMOND BURR

Godzilla first appeared in the movies in 1954. His monstrous size and loud roar still frighten people today.

DOGZILLA

Written and directed by
DAV PILKEY

Strategy Focus

The author calls this story "extremely goofy." Do you agree with him? **Evaluate** how well he uses words and pictures to make you feel this way.

The stars of *Dogzilla* are the author's pets.
No harm came to any of the animals during the making of this book.

Starring

FLASH
as the Big Cheese

RABIES
*as Professor
Scarlett O'Hairy*

*Special
appearance by*
DWAYNE
as the Soldier Guy

LEIA
as the Monster

EG	THIS BOOK HAS BEEN RATED EXTREMELY GOOFY
	Some material may be too goofy for grown-ups.

It was summertime in the city of Mousopolis,

and mice from all corners of the community had come together
to compete in the First Annual Barbecue Cook-Off.

As the cook-off got under way, smoke from the
hot grills lifted the irresistible scent of barbecue sauce
over the roof-tops of the city.

A gentle wind carried the mouth-watering smell
into the distance, right over the top of an ancient crater.
Before long, a strange and mysterious sound was heard:
"Sniff . . . sniff. Sniff . . . sniff sniff sniff sniff . . ."

All at once, the volcano began to tremble.

And suddenly, up from the very depths of the earth
came the most terrifying creature ever known to mousekind:
the dreadful Dogzilla!

Immediately, soldiers were sent out to stop the mighty beast. The heroic troops were led by their brave commanding officer, the Big Cheese.

"All right, you old fleabag," squeaked the Big Cheese, "get those paws in the air — you're coming with us!"

Without warning, the monstrous mutt breathed her horrible breath onto the mice.

318

"Doggy breath!" screamed the soldiers. "Run for your lives!"

"Hey, come back here," shouted the Big Cheese to his troops. "What are you, men or mice?"

"We're MICE," they squeaked.

"Hmmmm," said the Big Cheese, "you're *right!* . . . Wait for me!"

The colossal canine followed the soldiers back to Mousopolis, licking up all of the food in her path.

Afterward, Dogzilla wandered through the city streets, doing those things that come naturally to dogs.

Dogzilla chased cars — right off the freeway!
Dogzilla chewed furniture — and the furniture store as well.
And Dogzilla dug up bones — at the Museum of Natural History.

Meanwhile, the Big Cheese had organized an emergency meeting with one of the city's greatest scientific minds, Professor Scarlett O'Hairy.

"Gentlemice," said Professor O'Hairy, "this monster comes from prehistoric times. It is perhaps millions of years old."

"Maybe we could teach it to do something positive for the community," suggested the Big Cheese.

"I'm afraid not," said Professor O'Hairy. "You simply *can't* teach an old dog new tricks!

322

Dogzilla \ˈdôg· zi· lə\ *noun*
1: a big, hairy dog 2: of,
or relating to a big, hairy dog
adv. 3: big, hairy doggishness
[< P Latin *Ogzilladay*]

"If we're going to defeat this dog, we've got to *think* like a dog! We've got to find something that *all* dogs are afraid of — something that will scare this beast away from Mousopolis FOREVER!"

"I've got an idea," squeaked the Big Cheese. . . .

Within minutes, the mice had assembled at the center of town.

"All right, Dogzilla," shouted the Big Cheese, "no more
Mister Mice Guy — it's BATHTIME!"

Suddenly, a blast of warm, sudsy water hit Dogzilla with
tremendous force.

The panicking pooch let out a burst of hot, fiery breath,
and the chase was on!

324

The Big Cheese tried to catch up to the hot dog with all the relish he could muster.

Dogzilla hightailed it out of town, and back into the mouth of the ancient volcano.

"Well, I'll be dog-goned," squeaked the Big Cheese. "It worked!"

With the horrifying memory of the bubble bath etched in her mind forever, Dogzilla never again returned to Mousopolis.

Within a year, Mousopolis had rebuilt itself . . . just in time for the Second Annual Barbecue Cook-Off. The mice of Mousopolis fired up their grills, confident that they would never see or hear from Dogzilla again.

However, there was one thing they hadn't counted on . . .

Puppies!

MEET THE Author and Illustrator DAV PILKEY

Dav Pilkey has been playful all his life. When he was a baby, his parents would often hear him laughing in his sleep. When he got a little older and other kids were outside playing sports, Dav was inside drawing goofy pictures.

Today Pilkey spends his time making goofy books. One day while he was watching television, Leia, the dog, came charging into the room and knocked over a castle made out of blocks. "Leia looked like a silly monster who had just rampaged a city," Pilkey says. That smashing scene gave him the idea for *Dogzilla*.

Other books:
A Friend for Dragon, Dragon Gets By, Kat Kong

Internet

To find out more about Dav Pilkey, visit Education Place. **www.eduplace.com/kids**

Think About the Selection

1. How is Dogzilla like most real dogs? How is she not like a real dog?

2. How does thinking like a dog help the mice defeat Dogzilla?

3. What if bathtime hadn't scared Dogzilla away? What other plans could the Big Cheese have made to save Mousopolis?

4. What do you think will happen at the Second Annual Barbecue Cook-Off?

5. How would the story have been different if a colossal kitty had come out of the volcano instead of a dreadful dog?

6. **Connecting/Comparing** How does Dav Pilkey make this story so funny and incredible? Give examples from both the words and the pictures.

Persuading

Write a Movie Ad

Write an ad for a movie of *Dogzilla.* Draw an exciting scene from the story. Add the title and list the actors. Write sentences and quotations from people that will make others want to see the movie.

Tips

- Look at newspaper ads for ideas.
- Use colorful adjectives such as *greatest, silliest,* and *heroic.*

Math

Figure Out the Sale Price

Look at the picture of Gonzales's Furniture store on page 321. Then look at the original prices of the furniture in the chart below. If the sale price of each piece of furniture were half of the original price, how much would each one cost?

Bonus Figure out the sale price of the items if they were one-third off.

Item	Original Price
sofa	$60
nightstand	$30
easy chair	$36
dresser	$48
mirror	$18
lamp	$24

Listening and Speaking

Create Tongue Twisters

Find a phrase in the story in which each word has the same beginning sound. Use that phrase to write a whole sentence in which all the important words have that same beginning sound. Say your tongue twisters aloud as fast as possible.

Tips

- Before writing, make a list of words to choose from.
- Practice speaking slowly at first. Then speed up.

The dreadful Dogzilla did dozens of dirty deeds.

Internet

Post a Review

Paws up or paws down? Write a review of *Dogzilla* and post it on Education Place. **www.eduplace.com/kids**

Skill: How to Read a Diagram

1. **Identify** what the diagram shows.

2. **Predict** how it will be useful.

3. Read the **labels** to find out what information each part of the diagram gives you.

4. As you read, **look back** at the diagram to see how it helps you.

Go with the Flow!

by Anne Prokos

Contact
Red Hot Volcanoes?
Feel the Heat!

World's Largest Foot. Great Garbage. High-Tech TV

Millions of years ago, volcanoes started out as holes or cracks in the Earth's crust. After thousands of eruptions, layers of lava hardened on top of one another. The layers turned into mountains.

Build your own volcano!

What You Need

- Modeling clay
- Small empty can
- Piece of cardboard
- Baking soda
- Vinegar
- Teaspoon
- Glue
- Plastic houses from a board game

1 Mold clay into a volcano shape. Leave an opening at the top for the empty can.

Here's what goes on beneath those mountains.

Rocks called strata melt below the Earth's crust. Gases and burned rock mix together to make hot magma.

Pressure causes magma to shoot out of volcanic craters or vents. When magma reaches the Earth's surface, it's called lava.

Gas and ashes from burned rock separate from the lava. The ashes form a cloud and fall toward the Earth.

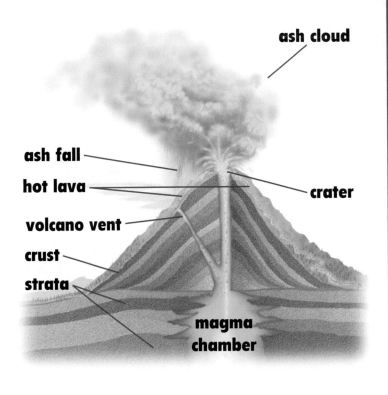

ash cloud

ash fall

hot lava

crater

volcano vent

crust

strata

magma chamber

 Insert the can into the "crater." Put your project on the cardboard and glue a few houses around your volcano.

3 Place one teaspoon of baking soda into the can. Add vinegar until it starts to foam. Watch where the "lava" flows.

333

A Story

A story tells about a true or fictional experience. It has a main character, and it has a beginning, a middle, and an end. Use this student's writing as a model when you write a story of your own.

Here I am with Pete.

> Introducing the **characters** in a story usually takes place at the beginning.

> A good description of the **setting** helps the reader to picture where the story takes place.

Pete, the Patriotic Pig

Pete was a patriotic pig. He said the Pledge of Allegiance every morning. He always dressed in red, white, and blue. His car was red, white, and blue too. Even his house was red, white, and blue.

Pete lived in Massachusetts. His job was to sing the National Anthem at the Boston Celtics basketball games. Everybody clapped and cheered after he sang. That made Pete feel really good.

One day Pete got bored with his job. He thought it would be fun to be an ice cream vendor instead.

So that day at the game he got the job to sell red, white, and blue ice cream. "Ice cream for sale! Ice cream for sale!" yelled Pete.

"My ice cream is melting!" screamed an angry fan.

"My ice cream is sour!" said another.

The job was not as much fun as Pete thought it would be. Nobody cheered for him or anything. Pete wanted his old job back.

The next day Pete got his old job back. He sang the National Anthem and everybody cheered. Pete was happy again.

A good **plot** makes the reader want to find out what will happen.

Using **dialogue** makes a story come alive.

A good **ending** wraps up the story.

Meet the Author

Eric D.

Grade: three

State: Massachusetts

Hobbies: soccer, reading

What he'd like to be when he grows up: a professional soccer player or a surgeon

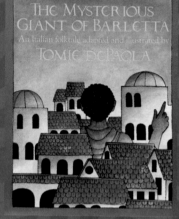

The Mysterious Giant of Barletta

Read to find the meanings of these words.

e • Glossary

giant

mysterious

pedestal

square

statue

weakling

A Mysterious STATUE

About 700 years ago, in 1309, a large **statue** of a young man washed up in the quiet harbor town of Barletta, Italy. No one knew where the statue had come from, but that didn't matter to the people of Barletta. They came to love the statue anyway.

Even today, the statue is **mysterious**. It stands on a **pedestal** in Barletta's town **square** and is almost eighteen feet tall. The statue looks strong and brave as it watches over the townspeople. The townspeople often tell stories about their beloved **giant**. One of their favorites is the story you are about to read.

This is the town of Barletta, Italy.

The mysterious giant watches over the town of Barletta from its pedestal in the square.

*Standing next to the giant makes a person look like a tiny **weakling**.*

Tomie dePaola

When Tomie dePaola was a boy, his Italian grandmother and Irish grandfather would tell him lots of old stories. As he listened, he began to dream of being an author. Today, in addition to writing his own stories, dePaola likes to retell old ones in his own words.

The Mysterious Giant of Barletta is one of those retellings. It is an Italian folktale. DePaola has retold Irish and Native American legends as well. Millions of children and adults enjoy the more than two hundred books he has illustrated and the nearly seventy he has written. To all his loyal fans, dePaola says "*grazie* — thank you."

OTHER BOOKS

Tony's Bread   *Strega Nona*

26 Fairmount Avenue   *Days of the Blackbird*

Jamie O'Rourke and the Big Potato

Internet

Visit Education Place and find out more about Tomie dePaola.
www.eduplace.com/kids

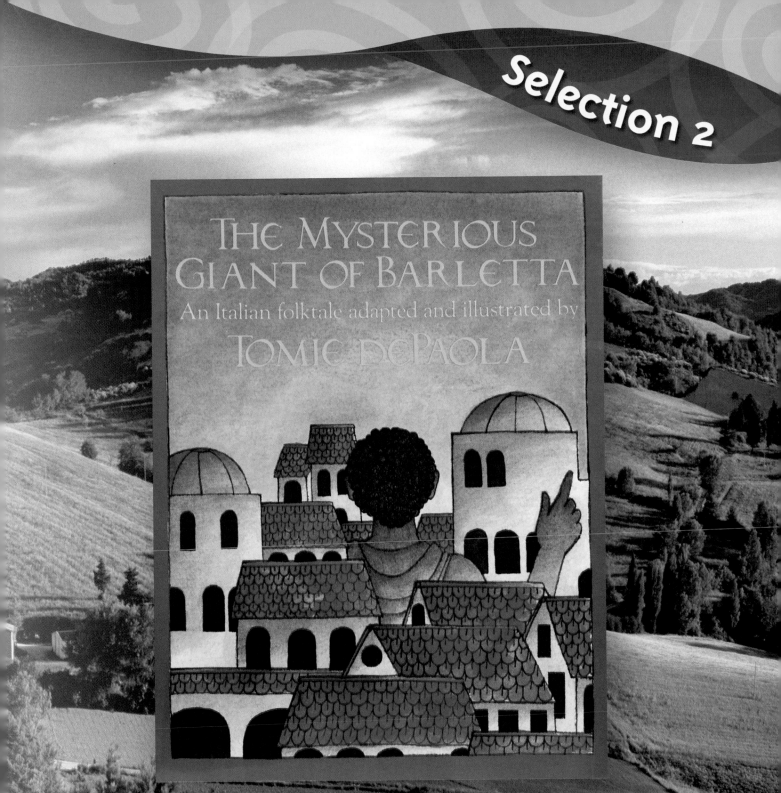

THE MYSTERIOUS
GIANT OF BARLETTA

An Italian folktale adapted and illustrated by

TOMIE DEPAOLA

★ Strategy Focus

As you read about Barletta and the giant,
think of **questions** about the town, its people,
and the strange events that happen there.

In the town of Barletta, in front of the Church of San Sepolcro, stood a huge statue. No one knew where it had come from or when. The Mysterious Giant — for that is what the people called the statue — had always been there as long as anyone could remember.

Even Zia Concetta [kahn-CHEHT-ta]. Zia Concetta was the oldest one in all of Barletta. She lived right across the square from the giant statue. "Every day, every night, for my whole lifetime, I've looked out the window and there he is," she would say.

341

Good weather and bad, the Mysterious Giant stood there. The people of Barletta loved having the statue in their town.

In the early morning, right before the sun came up, the sisters from the convent and other townspeople came to the church for Holy Mass. They always greeted the giant with a nod or a smile.

The people on the way to market always hailed the giant and asked that he give them good luck to sell all their goods or to get a good bargain.

All day long the children played around his legs, and the doves flew around his head. The young boys would sit on his big feet and tell jokes.

A little later the older boys would sit on the giant's feet to watch the older girls walk by. And at night, lovers would steal kisses in the giant's shadow.

Then the streets would be empty. Doves would settle on the giant's head and shoulders and arms and coo themselves to sleep, and Zia Concetta would open her window and call, "*Buona notte, Colosso* — good night, Big One."

This was the time the giant loved best. All was calm, all was still. *Ah, what a peaceful life,* the Mysterious Giant thought.

But one day this peaceful life was over. Word had reached the town that an army of a thousand men was destroying all the towns and cities along the lower Adriatic coast. And this army was heading straight for Barletta.

The townspeople ran through the streets in panic. No one in Barletta was ready for an army coming to destroy them. They had no generals, no captains. Why, they didn't even have any soldiers!

Shouts and screams echoed off the buildings. The night was lit by torches. All the peace and quiet was gone. No doves came to settle on the Mysterious Giant's shoulders, and Zia Concetta didn't call *"Buona notte"* from her window. The Mysterious Giant didn't like this at all.

The next morning was no better. It seemed as though everyone was at the church for Holy Mass, but there was no market. No one even smiled, let alone waved at the Mysterious Giant. No children played. Everyone rushed around, piling their belongings in carts and wagons. Everyone was getting ready to run from Barletta. Everyone except Zia Concetta — and the Mysterious Giant.

345

"*Colosso*," she said to the huge statue, "as long as I can remember you have stood here looking over this town and its people. Barletta loves you and I know you love Barletta. I wish you could do something to save us from this army. With your size, I'm sure you could frighten them away. Why don't you hop down from your pedestal?"

And that's just what the Mysterious Giant did!

"Now . . ." said Zia Concetta. They put their heads together and came up with an idea. "And a good one, too," said Zia Concetta.

347

The Mysterious Giant climbed back and stood still. "People of Barletta," Zia Concetta called. "Come quickly! Great news . . . *un miracolo* — a miracle — our giant is going to save us. Come!"

The people of Barletta gathered around. "Friends," Zia Concetta said, "our giant will go to meet this army himself! All you have to do is three things. First, bring me the biggest onion you can find. Second, stay completely out of sight. Hide under the bed, hide in the closet, hide in the cellar, hide in the attic, but stay out of sight. And third — don't ask any questions! Have faith in our Mysterious Giant."

Someone quickly brought an onion. "Now, hide!" shouted Zia Concetta, and everyone scurried off.

"Well, *Colosso*," said Zia Concetta as she sliced the onion in half, *"buona fortuna."* The Mysterious Giant took an onion half in each hand, once more stepped off the pedestal, and strode off to meet the army.

Three miles outside the city the Mysterious Giant sat down by the side of the road and held the onion pieces close to his eyes. Big tears began to run down his cheeks. The giant made loud sobbing noises.

What a sight the army saw as it came over the hill! "Halt," shouted the captain. The army halted. "What is that?" the captain whispered to one of his lieutenants.

"It looks like a giant boy — crying," answered the lieutenant.

"Well, we'll see about this," said the captain, marching off to where the Mysterious Giant sat.

"I am Captain Minckion," the captain declared. "We have come to destroy this town. Who are you, and what are you doing here crying? No tricks now — answer me!"

"Oh, sir," said the giant, sobbing, "I'm sitting out here, away from the town, because the other boys in school won't let me play with them. They say I'm too small. They pick on me all the time. They call me names, like *minuscolo* and *debole* — 'tiny' and 'weakling.' I'm always the last one chosen for games. Today they told me that if I tried to go to school they would beat me up. I hate being so small."

The giant sniffed loudly and blew the hats off the soldiers standing in front. The captain and the army stood dumbstruck. If this giant was a small boy that the others teased, then imagine what the rest of the people of this town were like.

"But someday, sir," the giant bellowed, "someday, I'll show them. I'm going to eat up all my pasta, and I'll grow big and strong, and then I'll be able to fight back."

The soldiers began to back away, trembling. The lieutenants gathered around the captain, who had backed away from the giant, too. There was only one thing to do. Captain Minckion and his lieutenants drew their swords. They held them in the air and shouted . . .

"About-face! Double time — march!" The army turned and fairly ran in the opposite direction of Barletta. The Mysterious Giant threw away the onion halves, dried his tears, and went back to the Church of San Sepolcro.

"They're gone," shouted Zia Concetta to the townspeople, as the giant climbed back on his pedestal once more. "The army is gone. You can come out now. The town has been saved. Our giant did it!"

Che bella festa! What a celebration was held that night!

But when it was over and the moon was high in the sky, the Mysterious Giant looked out over the sleeping town. Doves cooed themselves to sleep on his head and his shoulders.

Everything was calm, everything was still. Zia Concetta opened her window.

"*Buona notte, Colosso,*" she called, "and *grazie.*"

Think About the Selection

1. When all the townspeople get ready to run from Barletta, why is Zia Concetta the only one who doesn't panic?

2. Why do you think the Mysterious Giant decides to help Zia Concetta and the town?

3. Why does Zia Concetta ask the townspeople to stay out of sight? What might have happened if they hadn't followed her orders?

4. Why is it better for the Giant to trick the soldiers rather than to fight them?

5. If the Mysterious Giant came to *your* town, what could he help the people do?

6. **Connecting/Comparing** Suppose the Big Cheese from Mousopolis were in charge of saving Barletta. What might his plan have been?

Expressing

Write a Postcard

If you were visiting Barletta, what would you write to a friend? On one side of an index card, write your friend's address and a short message. Compare Barletta with your hometown. On the other side of the card, draw a scene from Barletta.

Tips

- To get started, list places and people in Barletta.
- Include your friend's name, street address, city, state, and ZIP code.

Make a Map

How well do you know Barletta? Draw a map of the town. Put the town square at the center. Show all the important places you read about in the story. Label the places clearly. Don't forget the statue of the Giant!

Bonus Make a mileage scale for your map.

Make an Italian Phrase Book

Write all the Italian words and phrases from the story on separate pieces of paper. Then put them in alphabetical order. Write the English meaning on each page and draw a picture that shows the meaning. Bind the pages together. *Buon divertimento!* Have fun!

Internet

Complete a Web Word Scramble

How fast can you unscramble a word? Test your skills on words from *The Mysterious Giant of Barletta*. Visit Education Place today!

www.eduplace.com/kids

357

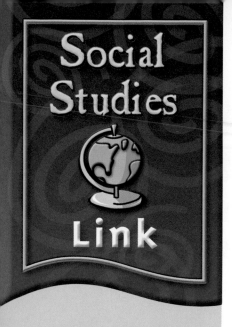
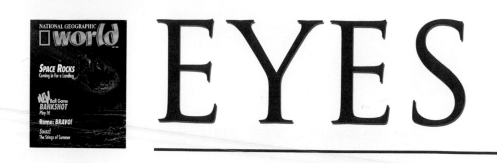

EYES

Where can you see ancient ruins, eat authentic spaghetti, and visit the Vatican, the world's smallest state, in one day? Head for Rome, Italy's capital. Grab your travel gear and *avanti* — "go."

Called the "Eternal City" because of its long history, Rome was founded, legend says, in 753 B.C. Later it was the seat of the Roman Empire. Today you'll find many remains of the past here. "There are lots of old monuments, statues, and museums," says Matteo Ferrucci, 13. "My favorite statue is one of the emperor Marcus Aurelius on his horse." Livia Bianchini, 13, favors monuments called obelisks. These tall stone pillars decorate many public spaces.

"There are so many different things to do in Rome that it's hard to get bored," says Francesco Pannarale, 12. "If you want to learn history, go to see the Colosseum and the Roman Forum. For a great view of the city, go to Zodiaco." That's a café on a hill in the northwest section of the city. "From Zodiaco you can see at least half of Rome," Francesco says. "There's also a *gelateria* [ice cream shop] there!"

on ROME

by M. Linda Lee

▲ **DWARFED** by a giant head and hand, Francesco examines part of a statue at the Conservators' Palace Museum in Rome, Italy, where he lives. "The pieces are huge," says Francesco. "I can imagine how the whole statue must have looked in ancient times."

359

What do Roman teens do for fun? "I often go to Luna Park with my friends or family," says Matteo. "Luna Park is an amusement park with lots of rides." Francesco, Livia, and Matteo all recommend the park at Villa Borghese [bohr-GAY-zay], a former 17th-century estate where you'll find museums, galleries, and a zoo. "There are great bike trails around the little lake," says Francesco. And you can go horseback riding.

No one can quite put a finger on what makes Rome so special. According to Matteo, who lived in New York City for several years, "Rome and New York both have interesting museums, but Rome has more history." Adds Francesco, "People come to Rome to see the old sights, but there are lots of modern things to see, too." Livia agrees. "Rome is *molto bella* [very beautiful]," she says. "It's the best city in the world!"

▼ TRUTH OR CONSEQUENCES. Bocca della Verità, the Mouth of Truth, puts Francesco to the test. An old legend says that the mouth will "bite" the hand of anyone who tells a lie.

Raising Dragons

WRITTEN BY
Jerdine Nolen

ILLUSTRATED BY
Elise Primavera

Raising Dragons

Read to find the meanings of these words.

e • Glossary

appetite

chores

harvested

hitched

plow

sown

tended

Working on the Farm

On a farm, there are many **chores** to do. Raising crops and taking care of all the animals is hard work. Before you read the story *Raising Dragons*, you might want to know what it's like to live on a real farm. Here are some things a good farmer does.

Farmers **plow** the soil with the help of tractors. This tractor is **hitched** to a special tool that breaks up the dirt.

This girl is feeding a calf. After she has **tended** this calf, she may have other animals to care for as well.

Seeds are **sown** over the ground. Once the seeds grow into plants, they must be tended until the crops are ready to pick.

After the crops are **harvested**, there is plenty of food to eat. That's just what you need when you've worked up a healthy **appetite** doing farm chores!

363

Meet the Author
JERDINE NOLEN

Where she grew up: Chicago, Illinois

Where she lives now: Ellicott City, Maryland

Where she gets her ideas for books: She says she gets them from her children, from her cats, and even while she's doing laundry.

Fun fact: Her book *Harvey Potter's Balloon Farm* was made into a TV movie.

Other books: *Harvey Potter's Balloon Farm, In My Momma's Kitchen, Irene's Wish*

Meet the Illustrator
ELISE PRIMAVERA

Where she grew up: Long Branch, New Jersey

Where she lives now: Monmouth Beach, New Jersey

First thing she learned to draw: A tree. Her brother taught her when she was six years old.

Where she gets her ideas for books: She says her best ideas come to her when she's in the shower.

Internet

Do you want to find out more about Jerdine Nolen and Elise Primavera? Try visiting Education Place.
www.eduplace.com/kids

Raising Dragons

WRITTEN BY
Jerdine Nolen

ILLUSTRATED BY
Elise Primavera

Strategy Focus

Use what you know about farms, animals, and make-believe to **predict** what might happen when a little girl tries to raise a dragon on her family's farm.

Pa didn't know a thing about raising dragons. He raised corn and peas and barley and wheat. He raised sheep and cows and pigs and chickens. He raised just about everything we needed for life on our farm, but he didn't know a thing about raising dragons.

Ma didn't know about dragons, either. She made a real nice home for us. But when it came to dragons, she didn't even know what they wanted for dessert!

Now me, I knew everything about dragons, and I knew they were real.

At first Pa thought the notion of dragons on a farm was just plain foolishness. "I'm not too particular about fanciful critters. And, I don't have any time for make-believe," he told me one day. So when Pa said he didn't want to talk anymore, I knew I'd better keep my opinions to myself. I did my chores with my thoughts in my head at one end of the barn while Pa worked at the other end with his thoughts.

I remember the day my life with dragons began. I was out for my Sunday-before-supper walk. Near Miller's cave I came across something that looked like a big rock. But it was too round and too smooth — not hard enough to be a rock.

Carefully I rolled it into the cave and went to fetch Pa.

"What do you think it is, Pa?"

"An egg. A big egg," was all he said. "Now you stay away from that thing, daughter. No telling what'll come out of it!" I couldn't tell if Pa was more scared than worried. "You just stay away, you hear me!" he said, pointing a finger.

I always minded my parents, never had a reason not to. And I tried to mind Pa now, but I could not stay away. Day after day I'd go to Miller's cave to wait and watch, and wonder: *What is coming out of that egg?*

One night I couldn't sleep. I got out of my bed and climbed out of my window onto the perch Pa had made for me in the oak tree.

But a loud noise broke the stillness of the night. *Crack!*
It was louder than one hundred firecrackers on the Fourth of
July. *CRACK!* I heard it again, this time louder than before.
It was coming from Miller's cave. At the first hint of dawn,
I headed toward that sound.

There in the corner of the cave, where I'd left it, was the
egg. And pushing its way out, like I've seen so many baby chicks
do, was a tiny dragon poking through that shell with its snout.

It was love at first sight.

"Hey there, li'l feller, welcome to the world," I sang, soft and
low. As I stroked his nose, a sweet little purring whimper came
from him. As I touched skin to scale, I knew I was his girl and he
was my dragon. I named him Hank.

Hank was just a joy to have around. He was a fire-breathing
dragon, and he made sure he kept his temper whenever I was near.

Pa wouldn't have seen the sense or the use of having a dragon
around who ate you out of house and home. Thankfully, Hank
preferred fish, frogs, eels, and insects to beef, lamb, chicken, and
pork. And he *did* have a healthy appetite!

Ma never wanted to know about Hank. Whenever I wanted to
talk about him, she'd cover her ears and sing. She said that having a
dragon around had to be worse than having a field full of critters.
But it wasn't.

Ma and Pa taught me about caring for living creatures from the day I was born. They taught me about raising lots of things, but they never imagined I would someday care for a critter most folks don't even believe existed. It did take a little time, but whether they liked it or not, Hank was part of our lives.

He was an awesome thing. Growing to be as big as the barn from tail to snout. Hank was very clumsy when his wings came in. But once he learned how to use them, we'd go flying, mostly at night.

Up until then I had been afraid of the dark. The shadows and muffled noises and the complete quiet stillness always seemed to be waiting and watching me. I had seen our farm from up in my tree perch. But Hank showed me my world from on high, the way a cloud or a bird or a star just might be seeing me. Up there I saw things for what they were. And it was just grand!

Pa was the first one to notice what he called a strangeness happening around our farm. One morning with Samson, our mule, hitched for work, Pa set out to plow the fields. But all the work had been done. The ground was turned over and seeds had been sown. Pa was plumb flabbergasted!

Hank and I tended the crops, too. We pulled weeds and kept varmints away. And Hank even got me to school before the first bell.

Even after all the good he'd done, Ma still didn't want any part of Hank. But when a hot spell hit, her tomatoes began to dry out. Hank hovered above them, fanning away the heat. He saved just about every last one of them. Ma didn't admit it, but she felt beholden to Hank. She began fixing fancy gourmet meals just for him — eel potpies, frog-leg pudding, and a fish-and-insect stew that Hank just loved.

Day by day Hank was getting bigger. Ma was uneasy about Hank's fire-breathing breath.

Pa paced with worry about all the corn Hank and I planted. There was corn growing *everywhere*. Ma cooked as much of it as she could, but there was too much. Just when it seemed like the corn would swallow up our farm, Hank grabbed Pa's shovel and dug a wide trench around the cornfield. Then he blew on it with his hot breath.

"What in tarnation?" Pa screamed. Ma ran out of the house carrying a bucket of water. But it was too late. The whole field was ablaze. We couldn't believe our ears — POP! POP!! Pop, Pop! POP! — or our eyes.

Hank was making popcorn. It took an entire week to salt and bag it. We sold it all — at a profit. It was the first dragon-popped popcorn anybody ever saw or tasted. Oh, it was *real* good, too.

When Ma harvested her tomatoes, Nancy Akins bought some. She claimed they had medicinal value. She said they cured her gout. Pretty soon folks wanted dragon-grown food like they wanted medicine. But there was nothing medicinal about it. It was just Hank.

379

The crowds and attention decided his fate. One evening Ma and I were sitting in front of our potbellied stove. She was shelling peas while I read *Murdoch's Adventure Atlas of the Known and Unknown World,* a book I'd gotten from the library that morning. In that instant I realized what I needed to do.

Come morning, Hank and I set out for the dragon-shaped landmass floating in the middle of the ocean.

There were dragons everywhere. They put us up in their best hotel, invited us to eat in their best restaurants. Hank felt right at home. When I saw Hank playing run-and-fly-and-chase, I knew he had found the perfect place to be.

All in all, it was a great vacation.

But at the end, it got real hard: I had to say farewell to Hank. At least for now.

Normally I don't get mushy at departing, but when Hank turned to me and called me Cupcake, I *boohooed* a heap.

Just as I was about to board my plane, Hank stood there on the runway trying to hide a wheelbarrow behind his back. His toothy grin lit up that cloudy day. That wheelbarrow was full of . . .

"ROCKS??" Ma squealed in puzzlement.

" 'Tain't rocks, Mother. They're eggs, dragon eggs!" I exclaimed. Pa beamed right proud.

Each egg looked different from the rest: One glowed, one glistened, another one flickered, and one even sparkled. I stood admiring the lot of them. Looking at those eggs, I thought about my Hank. For now, he was out there somewhere in the world. I knew I'd see him again. Wondering *when* was the only thing fixed in my mind.

But in the meantime, I knew what I had to do. The same way Pa knew that farming was in his blood, I knew that raising dragons was in mine.

There are some things you just know.

THINK ABOUT THE SELECTION

1. Describe the little girl's personality. What is she like? Give examples from the story to support your answer.

2. Why does Hank have to leave the farm? How do you think he felt about leaving?

3. If the little girl had never found the egg in Miller's Cave, how would life on the farm have been different?

4. What do you think will happen when the little girl tries to raise a group of dragons instead of just one?

5. What kind of person does someone have to be to take good care of an animal? Give examples from the story.

6. Connecting/Comparing Hank was very helpful on the farm. What might have happened if Hank were more like Dogzilla?

Narrating

WRITE A SEQUEL

A sequel to a story tells what happens after that first story ends. What might happen if the little girl went back to Dragon Island? What would she say to the dragons? Write a sequel using your ideas.

Tips

- Before writing, draw a picture of your ideas.
- Use quotation marks at the beginning and end of a person's exact words.

Science

MAKE A LIFE CYCLE CHART

Create a chart that shows the stages of Hank's life cycle. Begin with the egg that the little girl found. Draw pictures of the other stages in Hank's life.

Listening and Speaking

ROLE-PLAY A NEWS REPORT

In a small group, role-play a television reporter's news report from the farm. Decide who will be the reporter, the little girl, her parents, and Hank. Present the live interviews to the rest of the class.

Tips

- Watch a news report on TV for ideas.
- Prepare questions before doing the interviews.

Internet

TAKE AN ONLINE POLL

Have you ever raised a pet? What unusual pets do you or your friends have? Who is your favorite character in *Raising Dragons*? Take an Education Place online poll. **www.eduplace.com/kids**

Real-Life DRAGONS

by Robert Gray

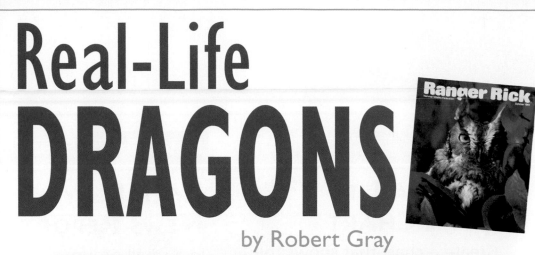

▲ FOREST DRAGON

You can see why this little lizard got the name "dragon." It has more spikes than most make-believe dragons! It lives in the rainforests of Australia.

Usually when forest dragons stay still, they're hard to see. Their green scales help to hide them in the leaves.

But when a forest dragon wants to scare an enemy, it stretches out the yellow skin under its chin. Then it fights with its teeth and claws.

Skill: How to Read a Science Article

Before you read . . .

1. **Read** the title, headings, and captions.

2. **Look at** the photos.

3. **Predict** what you will learn.

While you read . . .

1. **Identify** the main idea of each paragraph.

2. **Identify** special science words and facts.

3. **Take notes** to help you remember what you read.

The world's biggest lizards are also called dragons. No wonder — they can grow to be ten feet (three meters) long. And a Komodo almost looks as if it's breathing fire! As it walks along, its long forked tongue flicks in and out of its red mouth.

Komodos live on six tiny islands in Indonesia, a country north of Australia. Adult Komodos eat almost any small animal they can find, including smaller Komodo dragons.

And they're big enough to kill deer and water buffaloes, but they can't outrun them. Instead, they lie next to the animals' trails and strike out quickly to grab their prey.

If an animal gets away after being bitten, no problem. It will probably die in a day or two. That's because germs in the Komodo's saliva can cause a deadly infection. After the animal dies, it starts to smell rotten. And before long, a Komodo will follow the odor and find a delicious dead dinner.

With their spikes and scales and fierce looks, these real-life dragons are just AMAZING!

391

A lizard in the air? How rare! These dragons from India and Southeast Asia can't really fly. But they can glide from tree to tree to chase insects or escape from enemies.

Their "wings" are made of skin stretched over their ribs. To glide, they spread their ribs out and jump off a branch. The stretched-out skin acts like a parachute as they float down to a lower branch. When a flying dragon lands, it tucks its ribs against its body, as if it were closing a paper fan.

Both the green basilisk and the common basilisk have crests. That's why these dragon lizards were named after the rooster-like basilisks of long ago.

Make-believe basilisks were supposed to be able to kill people by looking at them. But these dragon lizards from Central America can do something amazing too. By running super-fast on their hind legs, they can zip across the top of the water for a short distance. What a great getaway!

Real or Make-Believe?

Which kind of dragons do you like best — the storybook dragons of long ago? Or the living lizards of today? You don't have to choose. You can have them all!

Real dragons are lurking in lots of zoos. Ask at a zoo's information desk if there are dragon lizards you can visit.

393

Background and Vocabulary

THE GARDEN OF ABDUL GASAZI

Written and Illustrated by CHRIS VAN ALLSBURG

The Garden of Abdul Gasazi

Read to find the meanings of these words.

e ● **Glossary**

awesome

convinced

disappeared

discovered

impossible

incredible

Unusual Gardens

People have enjoyed gardens for hundreds of years. To keep gardens private, people sometimes build fences or walls around them. When you walk inside the high stone walls of a formal garden, it's easy to be **convinced** that the rest of the world has **disappeared**.

In the world of gardens, nothing is **impossible**. Some gardeners create life-size mazes out of tall bushes and shrubs. Others cut and shape plants into **awesome**, larger-than-life animals. What would you do if you **discovered** a garden full of these animals? Would you walk right in? Take a chance, and enter *The Garden of Abdul Gasazi*.

A gardener's careful planning and clipping can create strange paths (above) and **incredible** leafy animals (below).

Meet the
Author and Illustrator
Chris Van Allsburg

Birthday: June 18

Favorite book as a child: *Harold and the Purple Crayon* by Crockett Johnson

Favorite subject in school: He loved art. Once, when he was sick, he wanted to go to school anyway because it was an art day.

His readers: He gets hundreds of letters from students. Some want a picture of him. Others want to invite him to dinner. They even ask him if he likes spaghetti.

His love of reading: He reads every word on the cereal box at breakfast, sometimes more than once.

Fun fact: His book *Jumanji* was made into a movie.

Other books:

Just a Dream
The Polar Express
Two Bad Ants
The Wreck of the Zephyr

Internet

You can find out more about Chris Van Allsburg at Education Place. **www.eduplace.com/kids**

THE GARDEN OF ABDUL GASAZI

Written and Illustrated by CHRIS VAN ALLSBURG

Strategy Focus

Strategy Focus

As you follow the trail of incredible events in the story, pause to **monitor** your understanding. Reread or read ahead to **clarify** any clues along the way.

397

Six times Miss Hester's dog Fritz had bitten dear cousin Eunice. So when Miss Hester received an invitation to visit Eunice she was not surprised to read "P.S., Please leave your dog home." On the day of her visit Miss Hester asked young Alan Mitz to stay with Fritz and give him his afternoon walk.

As soon as Miss Hester left, Fritz ran into the parlor. He loved to chew on the chairs and shake the stuffing out of the pillows. But Alan was ready. All morning long he kept Fritz from sinking his sharp little teeth into the furniture. Finally the dog gave up and fell asleep, exhausted. Alan took a nap, too, but first he hid his hat under his shirt, hats being one of Fritz's favorite things to chew.

An hour later Alan quickly awoke when Fritz gave him a bite on the nose. The bad-mannered dog was ready for his afternoon walk. Alan fastened Fritz's leash and the dog dragged him out of the house. Walking along, they discovered a small white bridge at the side of the road. Alan decided to let Fritz lead the way across.

Some distance beyond the bridge Alan stopped to read a sign. It said: ABSOLUTELY, POSITIVELY NO DOGS ALLOWED IN THIS GARDEN. At the bottom it was signed: ABDUL GASAZI, RETIRED MAGICIAN. Behind the sign stood a vine-covered wall with an open doorway. Alan took the warning quite seriously. He turned to leave, but as he did, Fritz gave a tremendous tug and snapped right out of his collar. He bolted straight ahead through the open door, with Alan running right behind.

401

"Fritz, stop, you bad dog!" cried Alan, but the dog simply ignored him. Down shadowed paths and across sunlit lawns they raced, deeper and deeper into the garden. Finally, Alan drew close enough to grab hold of Fritz. But as he reached out he slipped and fell. Fritz barked with laughter as he galloped out of sight. Alan slowly picked himself up. He knew he had to find Fritz before Mr. Gasazi discovered him. Bruised and tired, he hurried off in the dog's direction.

After a long search Alan was ready to give up. He was afraid he might never find Fritz. But then he came upon fresh dog prints. Slowly he followed Fritz's tracks along a path that led into a forest. The dirt path ended and a brick walk began. There were no more tracks to follow, but Alan was certain that Fritz must be just ahead.

Alan started running. In front of him he could see a
clearing in the forest. As he came dashing out of the woods he
stopped as quickly as if he had run up against a wall. For there,
in front of him, stood a truly awesome sight. It was the house of
Gasazi. Alan nervously climbed the great stairs, convinced Fritz
had come this way and been captured.

The boy's heart was pounding when he arrived at the huge door. He took a deep breath and reached for the bell, but before he touched it the door swung open. There, in the shadow of the hallway, stood Gasazi the Great. "Greetings, do come in" was all that he said.

Alan followed Gasazi into a large room. When the magician turned around Alan quickly apologized for letting Fritz into the garden. He politely asked that, if Mr. Gasazi had Fritz, would he please give him back? The magician listened carefully and then, smiling, said, "Certainly you may have your little Fritzie. Follow me." With those words he went to the door and led Alan back outside.

They were walking across the lawn when suddenly Gasazi stopped by a gathering of ducks. He began to speak in a voice that was more like a growl. "I detest dogs. They dig up my flowers, they chew on my trees. Do you know what I do to dogs I find in my garden?"

"What?" whispered Alan, almost afraid to hear the answer.

"I TURN THEM INTO DUCKS!" bellowed Gasazi.

In horror, Alan looked at the birds in front of him. When one duck came forward, Gasazi said, "There's your Fritz." Alan begged the magician to change Fritz back. "Impossible," he answered, "only time can do that. This spell may last years or perhaps just a day. Now take your dear bird and please don't come again."

When Alan took the bird in his arms it tried
to give him a bite. "Good old boy," said Alan sadly
as he patted the bird on the head. "You really
haven't changed so much." With tears in his eyes
he started for home. Behind him Alan could hear
Gasazi laughing. As he approached the stairway,
a gust of wind took Alan's hat sailing right off his
head. Running along with one arm reaching for the
hat, Alan lost his hold on Fritz. The duck flew out
ahead and grabbed the hat in midair. But instead
of landing he just kept on flying, higher and higher,
until he disappeared in the afternoon clouds.

Alan just stood and stared at the empty sky.
"Goodbye, old fellow," he called out sadly, sure that
Fritz was gone forever. At least he had something
to chew on. Slowly, one step after another, Alan
found his way back to the garden gate and over the
bridge. It was sunset by the time he reached Miss
Hester's. Lights were on and he knew she must be
home. With a heavy heart he approached the door,
wondering how Miss Hester would take the news.

When Miss Hester came to the door Alan blurted out his incredible story. He could barely hold back the tears; then, racing out of the kitchen, dog food on his nose, came Fritz. Alan couldn't believe his eyes. "I'm afraid Mr. Gasazi played a trick on you," said Miss Hester, trying to hide a smile. "Fritz was in the front yard when I returned. He must have found his own way home while you were with Mr. Gasazi. You see, Alan, no one can really turn dogs into ducks; that old magician just made you think that duck was Fritz."

Alan felt very silly. He promised himself he'd never be fooled like that again. He was too old to believe in magic. Miss Hester watched from the porch as Alan waved goodbye and hurried down the road to go home. Then she called out to Fritz, who was playfully running around the front yard. He came trotting up the front steps with something in his mouth and dropped it at Miss Hester's feet. "Why you bad dog," she said. "What are you doing with Alan's hat?"

413

Think About the Selection

1. How would you describe Abdul Gasazi's personality? Use details from the story to make your point.

2. How do you think Fritz the dog ended up with Alan's hat?

3. Why does Miss Hester believe that Abdul Gasazi has played a trick on Alan? Do you agree with her?

4. How does Chris Van Allsburg make this story seem so mysterious? Give examples from the story.

5. Do you think Alan will ever go back into Abdul Gasazi's garden? Would *you* go into the garden if given the chance? Explain your answers.

6. **Connecting/Comparing** Compare Dragon Island in *Raising Dragons* to Abdul Gasazi's garden.

Reflecting

Write a Journal Entry

What a day Alan had! Write Alan's journal entry about his day with Fritz. Be sure to tell how he feels about Fritz, Abdul Gasazi, and all the day's strange events. Use exciting and mysterious details from the story.

Tips
- Before writing, make a list of the main events.
- Start the entry with a day and a date.

414

Role-Play a Dialogue

What if a dog you were taking care of ran into Abdul Gasazi's garden? With a partner, role-play a dialogue between yourself and Abdul Gasazi. What reasons could you give for getting the dog back? What would Abdul Gasazi say? Will you get back a dog or something else? You decide!

BUT THIS IS NOT MY DOG!

Tips

- Write out your dialogue first.
- Practice with your partner.

Compare Van Allsburg's Art

Choose a picture from *The Garden of Abdul Gasazi* and a picture from another book by Chris Van Allsburg. Compare the pictures. How are they alike? What can you tell about Van Allsburg's style from these pictures? Write your ideas and share them with the class.

from *The Stranger* by Chris Van Allsburg

Internet

Complete a Web Maze

Can you find your way out of Abdul Gasazi's garden? Print a maze from Education Place and try your luck. **www.eduplace.com/kids**

Skill: How to Read an Interview

❶ **Read** the title and the introduction.

❷ **Identify** who is being interviewed and who is asking the questions.

❸ **Ask** yourself what you know about the person being interviewed.

❹ As you read, **pause** to make sure you understand each question and answer.

Enter the World of CHRIS VAN ALLSBURG

by Stephanie Loer

The questions for this interview with Chris Van Allsburg came from students, teachers, and fans of his books.

Where do you get the ideas for your pictures and stories?

At first, I see pictures of a story in my mind. Then creating the story comes from asking questions of myself. I guess you might call it the "what if — and what then" approach to writing and illustration.

Polar Express started with the idea of a train standing alone in the woods. Then I began asking questions: What if a boy gets on the train? What does he do? Where does he go? After the boy got on, I tried different destinations out in my mind. What about north? Who lives in the north? Then ideas of Christmas, Santa Claus, and faith began to take shape.

Van Allsburg's ideas come to life in his sketches.

How long does it take you to write and illustrate a book?

I begin thinking about the idea. Then I come up with the pictures and the story — in my mind. The next step is putting the illustrations and story down on paper. At that point, it becomes intense work — all day, every day, even on weekends. From the time I come up with the idea, do the book, and deliver it to the printers, it takes about seven months.

Van Allsburg created sketches for his book *Jumanji*. Then he drew a complete outline (above) of each sketch and turned it into a finished illustration (right).

417

An ordinary train looks mysterious in this illustration from Van Allsburg's book *The Polar Express.*

How would you describe the artistic style in your books?

Think of it this way: Although the pictures look quite representational — like everyday, ordinary things — underlying this orderly look of the drawings there is a somewhat mysterious or puzzling quality.

In other words, the style I use allows me to make a drawing that has a little mystery to it, even if the actual things I am drawing are not strange or mysterious.

If you were to do a sequel, what books would you select?

My own interests might draw me to *The Widow's Broom,* because the widow and the broom could have some more adventures. Also, *Two Bad Ants* might get in trouble again in a different room. Or Alan could go back to Gasazi and get into more trouble with the magician.

So, I guess if I ever do run out of ideas — there's lots of material to fall back on. But I doubt if that will ever happen.

Van Allsburg started collecting plastic animals when he needed good models for *Jumanji.*

418

Focus on Fritz

No talk with Chris Van Allsburg would be complete without Fritz. While Chris does not own a dog, his brother-in-law once owned an English bull terrier very similar to Fritz. That dog (see below) served as an inspiration for *The Garden of Abdul Gasazi*. Since then, Fritz has appeared in almost all of Chris Van Allsburg's books, though sometimes he is hiding.

Can you find Fritz in every book? We don't want to give away all of Fritz's hiding places, but we will get you started. In *The Polar Express*, he is the puppet on the bedknob on the first page. Sorry, no more hints, but if you look close enough, you'll eventually find Fritz.

Enjoying the Backyard

Check Your Progress

Incredible events happened in all four stories in this theme. Now you will read two more incredible stories and compare them with the others. You will also practice your test-taking skills.

Before you begin, think about where Jerdine Nolen gets her ideas for incredible stories. Where do you think the other authors in this theme got their ideas?

The first selection you're about to read really happened. The second selection is a fantasy. As you read, ask yourself what makes them both incredible.

Read and Compare

Find out what happens to two pigs on the loose.

Try these strategies:
Monitor and Clarify
Summarize

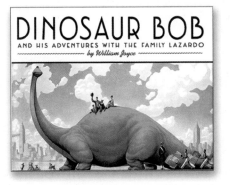

A dinosaur comes to live with a family in New York.

Try these strategies:
Question
Predict and Infer

Strategies in Action *Always use your reading strategies while you read.*

FUGITIVES ON FOUR LEGS

by Jean Kaplan Teichroew
photographs by Patrick Ward

When two pigs make a run for freedom, the world notices.

THEY ACTED LIKE PIGS. Yet people loved and honored them. Butch and Sundance, two Tamworth pigs, ended up having an excellent adventure on the day they were supposed to go to market. They managed to wiggle free of the butcher and begin life on the run in Malmesbury, England. Fleeing police and animal workers for more than a week, the pair pigged out on apples, worms, and roots. By the time they were captured, the pigs were international celebrities.

During the pigs' escapade, people rooted for their safety. Updates of their adventures appeared in newspapers and on television in Europe and the United States. In England the *London Daily Mail* bought the pair for thousands of dollars, promising the concerned public that the pigs would never become pork. And now?

The pigs are living the quiet life at an animal sanctuary. And as celebrities, they often wallow in their luxurious life.

DINOSAUR BOB

AND HIS ADVENTURES WITH THE FAMILY LAZARDO

~~~ written and illustrated by William Joyce ~~~

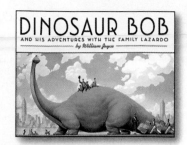

THE LAZARDOS were an interesting family. Every year, before the start of baseball season, they'd take a trip far from their beloved home in Pimlico Hills.

"Travel is adventure. Adventure makes you homesick, and baseball makes everything A-OK," explained Dr. Lazardo.

The Lazardos always returned from their journeys with some amazing treasure.

"I wonder what they'll drag back this time?" groused jealous Mrs. DeGlumly, the mayor's wife.

The Lazardos zipped about from one spot on the globe to another: London, Rome, Zanzibar, Cleveland.

While they were on safari in Africa, young Scotty Lazardo wandered away from camp and returned with a dinosaur.

"Look what I caught!" he said.

"Can we keep him?" pleaded Scotty's sisters, Zelda and Velma.

"I don't see why not," said Dr. Lazardo.

"He looks kind of like my Uncle Bob," said Mrs. Lazardo.

Jumbu, their bodyguard, said nothing.

Scotty patted the dinosaur on the nose. "Bob?" he tried.

The dinosaur smiled and wagged his giant tail.

So they named him Bob.

    With Bob along safari life was fun. They settled into a routine: swimming in the morning, games of baseball in the afternoon, and songs by the campfire before bed.

    One night, after a rousing rendition of "The Hokey Pokey," Mrs. Lazardo remarked, "Dancing and dinosaurs, who could ask for anything more?"

One day while deep in the jungle, they came to the banks of the river Nile. Dr. Lazardo said, "Let's go sailing!"

So they made Bob into a ship and steered him down the river. "Going by Bob is the only way to travel," sighed Zelda. Everyone began to sing "Take Me Out to the Ball Game." Bob hummed along. Jumbu said nothing but tapped his foot. It was grand.

Bob and the Lazardos were becoming quite attached to one another. But they couldn't sail him all the way back to Pimlico Hills.

"Bob took us down the Nile in style," reasoned the doctor. "It would be bad manners if we didn't return the favor."

So Dr. Lazardo booked passage on a luxury liner. Passengers danced the conga up and down Bob's back while he played his trumpet—a gift from the ship's orchestra.

"I think he likes the trumpet," said Scotty.

"I'll write him a song," said Zelda.

Every evening, the children led Bob up to his berth in the ship's smokestacks and brought him a bedtime snack—two peanut-butter-and-bologna sandwiches and four hundred double Dutch chocolate cakes. After a serenade of Zelda's special song, "The Ballad of Dinosaur Bob," Bob always fell asleep with a smile on his face.

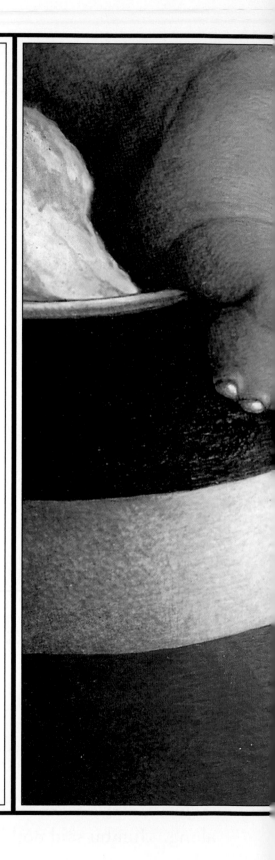

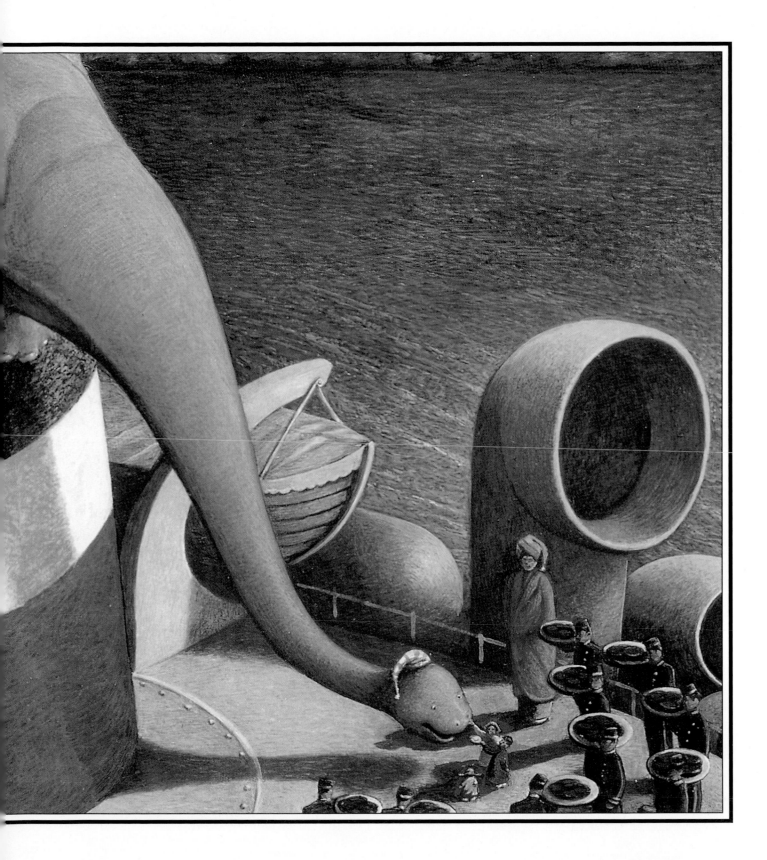

Their arrival in New York was quite eventful. Tugboats blew their whistles, freighters blasted their horns, people waved from bridges.

"New York loves a show," said Mrs. Lazardo.

"And Bob's the biggest show in town," said Dr. Lazardo as they gathered up their baggage.

They toured New York, and after a light lunch of 7,500 hot dogs in Central Park, they caught a train to Pimlico Hills. It was Bob's first train ride.

When they arrived in Pimlico Hills, traffic stopped. Dogs barked. People squealed with delight. Mrs. DeGlumly, the mayor's wife, turned pea green with envy.

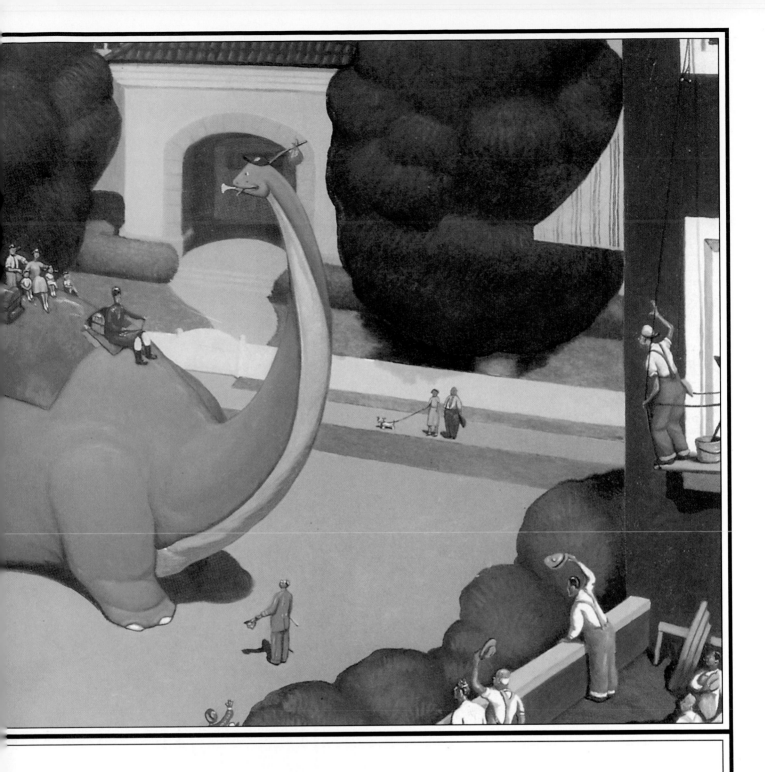

"That thing's a menace to the community!" she grumped.
"I think he's kinda nice," said the mayor meekly.
The Lazardos began to sing "Pimlico Hills, My Home
Town." Bob played his trumpet. The whole town sang along.

Reporters flocked to the Lazardos' house.

"Bob will scare off burglars," Dr. Lazardo told them.

"And he can blow a mean trumpet," said Zelda.

"He Hokey Pokeys like a fool," said Velma.

"And can he play **baseball**!" shouted Scotty.

Jumbu said nothing.

The photographers' cameras flashed. LENGTHY LIZARD LANDS WITH LAZARDOS read the headline in the paper.

Bob was famous.

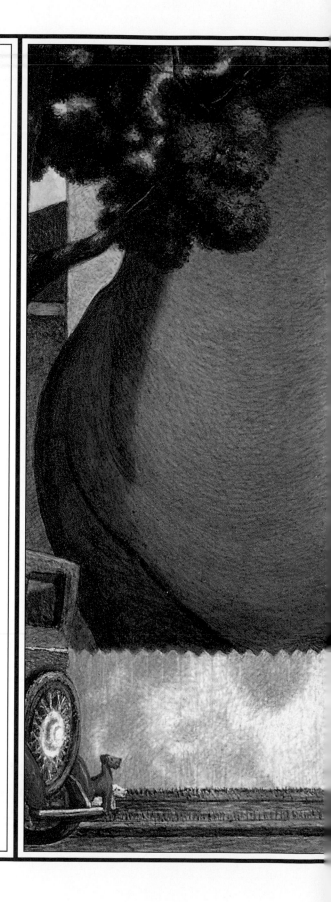

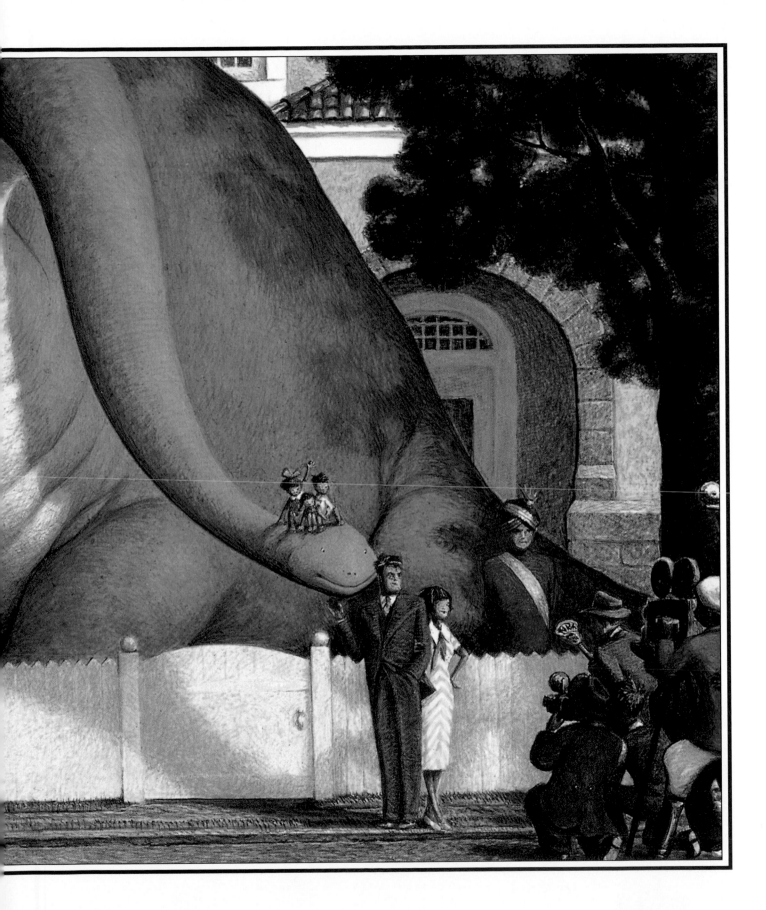

The Ballad of Dinosaur Bob

by Zelda Lazardo

(to the tune of "Auld Lang Syne")

Moderately

He's Bob, the best old Bob, the big-gest Bob you've ev-er seen. He's Me- so-zo-ic

and he- ro- ic, and he's real-ly green. Yes, large and green and so se-rene, he's

gen- tle and he's sweet, and when the mu- sic plays for him he __ stamps his migh- ty feet. He's

Bob, the best old Bob, the big-gest Bob you'll ev - er know. He's

Me- so- zo- ic and he- ro- ic, and we love him so.

Think and Compare

Fugitives on Four Legs
by Jean Kaplan Teichroew

1. Think about Dinosaur Bob and the pigs in "Fugitives on Four Legs." Why did the people in each selection care about them?

2. Can an author make a reader believe an incredible story? Use examples from the selections to explain.

3. The Lazardos keep Dinosaur Bob, but the little girl in *Raising Dragons* takes Hank back to Dragon Island. Why do you think they make different choices?

4. Think about one of the incredible stories in the theme. What do you think would happen next?

Strategies in Action How did using reading strategies help you read better during this theme?

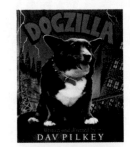

Write a Lost-and-Found Ad

Create a poster describing an incredible pet you have lost or found. It can be a make-believe animal or a wild animal. Draw a picture and write a short description of the pet.

Tips

- Use adjectives to describe what the pet looks or sounds like.
- List unusual habits the pet has.
- Include your phone number.

Writing a Personal Response

Some tests may ask you to write about your thoughts and experiences and connect them to what you have read. Here is a sample question for *Incredible Stories*.

Write your answer to this question.

Fantasy stories are often based on events that could happen in real life. Which story event in this theme is most like something that might happen in your life? Explain.

1 Understand the question.

Find the key words. Use them to understand what you need to do. Decide what to write about.

2 Get ready to write.

Look back at the selection. List details that answer the question. Think about yourself. List thoughts and experiences that answer the question.

Here's a sample chart.

Story Details	My Experiences
Dogzilla chews furniture. Dogzilla is really big. Dogzilla knocks things over.	Gruffly sleeps on the couch. He weighs more than 100 pounds. Things in my house can break.

Write your answer.

Use details from both of your lists. Write a clear and complete answer.

Now look at this sample answer.

> When Dogzilla chewed up the furniture and knocked things over, I thought of my dog, Gruffly. My parents own a really soft couch that Gruffly likes to sleep on. If he ever chewed that it would make a big mess. Dogzilla also made a big mess. Gruffly is really big, like Dogzilla. If he walked into the shelf that holds my grandmother's plates, he might knock them over and make a really big mess without trying to.

This glossary contains meanings and pronunciations for some of the words in this book. The Full Pronunciation Key shows how to pronounce each consonant and vowel in a special spelling. At the bottom of the glossary pages is a shortened form of the full key.

Full Pronunciation Key

Consonant Sounds

b	**bib**, ca**bb**age	kw	**ch**oir, **qu**ick	t	**t**igh**t**, stopp**ed**
ch	**ch**ur**ch**, sti**tch**	l	**l**id, need**l**e, ta**ll**	th	ba**th**, **th**in
d	**d**ee**d**, mail**ed**, pu**dd**le	m	a**m**, **m**an, du**mb**	*th*	ba**the**, **th**is
f	**f**ast, **f**i**fe**, o**ff**, **ph**rase, rou**gh**	n	**n**o, sudd**en**	v	ca**ve**, val**ve**, **v**ine
		ng	thi**ng**, i**nk**	w	**w**ith, **w**olf
g	**g**a**g**, **g**et, fin**g**er	p	**p**o**p**, ha**pp**y	y	**y**es, **y**olk, on**i**on
h	**h**at, **wh**o	r	**r**oa**r**, **rh**yme	z	ro**se**, si**ze**, **x**ylophone, **z**ebra
hw	**wh**ich, **wh**ere	s	mi**ss**, **s**au**ce**, **sc**ene, **s**ee	zh	gara**ge**, plea**s**ure, vi**s**ion
j	**j**u**dg**e, **g**em	sh	di**sh**, **sh**ip, **s**ugar, ti**ss**ue		
k	**c**at, **k**ick, s**ch**ool				

Vowel Sounds

ă	p**a**t, l**au**gh	ŏ	h**o**rrible, p**o**t	ŭ	c**u**t, fl**oo**d, r**ou**gh, s**o**me
ā	**a**pe, **ai**d, p**ay**	ō	g**o**, r**ow**, t**oe**, th**ough**	û	c**i**rcle, f**u**r, h**ea**rd, t**e**rm, t**u**rn, **u**rge, w**o**rd
â	**ai**r, c**a**re, w**ea**r	ô	**a**ll, c**au**ght, f**o**r, p**aw**		
ä	f**a**ther, k**o**ala, y**a**rd	oi	b**oy**, n**oi**se, **oi**l		
ĕ	p**e**t, pl**e**asure, **a**ny	ou	c**ow**, **ou**t	yŏŏ	c**u**re
ē	b**e**, b**ee**, **ea**sy, p**ia**no	ŏŏ	f**u**ll, b**oo**k, w**o**lf	yōō	**a**b**u**se, **u**se
ĭ	**i**f, p**i**t, b**u**sy	ōō	b**oo**t, r**u**de, fr**ui**t, fl**ew**	ə	**a**go, sil**e**nt, penc**i**l, lem**o**n, circ**u**s
ī	r**i**de, b**y**, p**ie**, h**igh**				
î	d**ea**r, d**ee**r, f**ie**rce, m**e**re				

Stress Marks

Primary Stress ´: bi·ol·o·gy [bī **ŏl´** ə jē]
Secondary Stress ´: bi·o·log·i·cal [bī´ ə **lŏj´** ĭ kəl]

A

an·ces·tor (ăn´ sĕs´ tər) *noun*
A person one's family comes from: *Helen and her parents were born in the United States, but their **ancestors** were born in China.*

ap·pe·tite (ăp´ ĭ tīt´) *noun*
The desire for food: *The larger the puppy grew, the bigger its **appetite** became.*

ar·mor (är´ mər) *noun* A heavy covering, often of metal, worn to protect the body in battle: *The soldier put on **armor** before the battle began.*

awe·some (ô´ səm) *adjective*
Causing a feeling of wonder, fear, and respect: *John was amazed by the **awesome** sight of the old castle.*

B

be·lay (bĭ lā´) *noun* An object or a person that a climber's rope can be tied to for safety: *Kit felt safe climbing down the rock because her mother was on **belay**.*

bor·der (bôr´ dər) *noun*
A part that forms the outside edge of something: *There was a lace **border** around the edge of the tablecloth.*

C

chore (chôr) *noun* A small job, usually done on a regular schedule: *Rachel's daily **chores** include washing the dishes and walking the dog.*

col·lec·tion (kə lĕk´ shən) *noun* A group of objects gathered together and saved, sometimes for display or study: *Paul has a **collection** of coins from around the world.*

co·los·sal (kə lŏs´ əl) *adjective*
Very big; enormous: *An elephant is **colossal** compared to a mouse.*

com·rade (kŏm´ răd´) *noun*
A companion, especially one who shares one's activities: *Rosa's **comrades** on the swim team cheered when she won the race.*

con·ga (kŏng´ gə) *noun* A tall, narrow drum played by striking with the hands: *The musician played the **conga** at my cousin's wedding.*

con·vince (kən vĭns´) *verb*
To cause to do or believe something; to make feel certain: *Because the door was open, Sasha was **convinced** that his little sister had been in his room.*

crea·ture (krē´ chər) *noun*
A living being, especially an animal: *Ruth's pet dog is a friendly **creature**.*

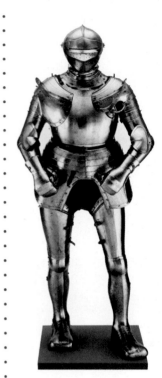

armor

Comrade
Spanish soldiers used to live in rooms called *camaradas.* Soldiers who shared a room called each other *camaradas.* In time, this became the English word *comrade.*

oo **boo**t / ou **ou**t / ŭ **cu**t / û **fu**r / hw **wh**ich / th **thi**n / *th* **th**is / zh vi**s**ion / ə **a**go, sil**e**nt, penc**i**l, lem**o**n, circ**u**s

441

D

de·scent (dĭ **sĕnt´**) *noun* The act of moving downward: *The plane lowered its wheels as it continued its **descent** to the ground.*

di·rec·tion (dĭ **rĕk´** shən) *noun* The line or path along which someone or something goes, lies, or points: *The road split in three different **directions**.*

dis·ap·pear (dĭs ə **pîr´**) *verb* To pass out of sight; vanish: *The sky became dark when the sun **disappeared** behind some clouds.*

dis·cov·er (dĭ **skŭv´** ər) *verb* To find or learn: *When Eric moved the branch, he **discovered** a nest of birds in the tree.*

E

el·der (ĕl´ dər) *noun* A person who is older: *Seth's grandmother and grandfather are the **elders** in the family.*

em·broi·der (ĕm **broi´** dər) *verb* To decorate by sewing designs with a needle and thread: *The red flowers were **embroidered** on the cloth.*

en·dure (ĕn **dŏŏr´**) *or* (ĕn **dyŏŏr´**) *verb* To put up with; to bear: *Julia **endured** the rain and cold during her camping trip.*

F

fare·well (fâr **wĕl´**) *noun* Good wishes at parting: *Jared said **farewell** to his neighbors before he left for vacation.*

flour·ish (flûr´ ĭsh) *noun* An energetic or dramatic waving motion: *Scott unrolled the new flag with a **flourish**.*

G

gath·er·ing (gă*th*´ ər ĭng) *noun* A coming together of people: *The family **gathering** included parents, grandparents, and children.*

gi·ant (jī´ ənt) *noun* A huge, very strong, imaginary creature that looks like a human being. *—adjective* Extremely large; huge: *The **giant** pizza was big enough to feed twenty people.*

H

har·ness (här´ nĭs) *noun* A set of leather straps and metal pieces used to keep a person or animal in place: *The woman held the guide dog close by its **harness**.*

har·vest (här´ vĭst) *verb* To gather or pick: *We **harvested** the ripe apples from our tree and baked an apple pie.*

Elder
Elder comes from the same Old English word as *old*.

embroider

harvest

ă rat / ā **pay** / â **care** / ä **father** / ĕ **pet** / ē **be** / ĭ **pit** / ī **pie** / î **fierce** / ŏ **pot** / ō **go** / ô **paw, for** / oi **oil** / ŏŏ **book**

L

he·ro·ic (hĭ **rō´** ĭk) *adjective* Very brave or daring: *The firefighter was famous for his **heroic** rescues.*

hitch (hĭch) *verb* To tie or fasten: *We **hitched** our horse, Fred, to the wagon so he could pull it.*

hon·or (ŏn´ ər) *noun* Special respect for excellence. *—verb* To show special respect for: *We will **honor** our teacher by giving her an award.*

hor·ri·fy·ing (hôr´ ə fī´ ĭng) *adjective* Causing much fear: *I liked riding the roller coaster, but Kevin thought it was **horrifying**.*

I

im·i·tate (ĭm´ ĭ tāt´) *verb* To copy the actions, looks, or sounds of: *Anna learned the dance by **imitating** her sister.*

im·pos·si·ble (ĭm **pŏs´** ə bəl) *adjective* Not able to happen or exist: *It is **impossible** to turn straw into gold.*

in·cred·i·ble (ĭn **krĕd´** ə bəl) *adjective* **1.** Too unlikely to be believed. **2.** Astonishing or amazing: *No one would believe Leah's **incredible** story about a talking fish.*

ledge (lĕj) *noun* A flat space like a shelf on the side of a cliff or rock wall: *The rock climber rested on a **ledge** halfway up the cliff.*

M

mon·strous (mŏn´ strəs) *adjective* Extremely large; enormous: *The rowboat looked tiny next to the **monstrous** ship.*

mys·te·ri·ous (mĭ **stîr´** ē əs) *adjective* Very hard to explain or understand: *No one could explain the **mysterious** egg on the teacher's desk.*

N

nee·dle (nēd´ l) *noun* A small, thin tool for sewing. It has a sharp point at one end and a tiny hole called an *eye* at the other end to put thread through: *He used a **needle** and thread to fix the hole in his sock.*

P

ped·es·tal (pĕd´ ĭ stəl) *noun* A base or support, as for a column or statue: *The Statue of Liberty stands on top of a **pedestal**.*

hitch

needle

ōō b**oo**t / ou **ou**t / ŭ c**u**t / û f**u**r / hw **wh**ich / th **th**in / *th* **th**is / zh vi**si**on / ə **a**go, sil**e**nt, penc**i**l, lem**o**n, circ**u**s

per·cus·sion (pər **kŭsh´** ən) *noun* A kind of musical instrument, such as a drum, that is played by striking or shaking: *The audience clapped to the beat of the* **percussion** *section.*

per·form (pər **form´**) *verb* To present, usually in front of an audience: *Many actors begin* **performing** *when they are children.*

plow (plou) *verb* To break up and turn over the soil with a special tool: *The farmer had to* **plow** *the fields before planting seeds.*

plow

R

rap·pel (ră **pĕl´**) *verb* To move down a cliff or the side of a mountain, using a rope attached to a rock and to a harness for safety: *The rock climbers* **rappel** *down the cliff, using short jumps.*

rec·ord (**rĕk´** ərd) *noun* A disk on which music is stored for listening: *Ann played the band's* **record** *over and over.*

re·spect (rĭ **spĕkt´**) *noun* Admiration or consideration: *Brian showed his* **respect** *for nature by helping to clean up the beach.* —*verb* To have or show respect for.

sow

roy·al·ty (**roi´** əl tē) *noun* Members of a royal family, such as kings, queens, princes, or princesses: *The country's* **royalty** *lived in the castle.*

rum·pled (**rŭm´** pəld) *adjective* Wrinkled: *Anita shook out her* **rumpled** *coat after sitting on it during the concert.*

S

sal·sa (**säl´** sə) *noun* A type of dance music that comes from Latin America: *Juan likes to play the trumpet when he listens to* **salsa** *music.*

scraps (skrăps) *noun* Leftover bits of cloth or other material: *Manuel used* **scraps** *of colored paper to create a picture.*

sew (sō) *verb* To make, repair, or fasten something with stitches, using a needle and thread: *Suki's mother had* **sewn** *Suki a bear costume for the school play.*

sit·u·a·tion (sĭch´ o͞o **ā´** shən) *noun* A set of conditions at a certain moment in time: *Freezing rain or thick fog can create dangerous* **situations** *for people who drive to work.*

sow (sō) *verb* To scatter seed over the ground for growing: *The seeds Amir had* **sown** *in the garden grew into pumpkins.*

ă rat / ā **pay** / â **care** / ä **father** / ĕ **pet** / ē **be** / ĭ **pit** / ī **pie** / î **fie**rce / ŏ **pot** / ō **go** / ô **paw, for** / oi **oil** / o͞o b**ook**

square (skwâr) *noun* An open area in a city or town where two or more streets meet: *Jacob and Tony ate their lunch on a bench in the town square.*

stat·ue (stăch′ ōō) *noun* An image, often of a person or an animal, made out of something solid, such as stone or metal: *Gina saw a huge statue of Abraham Lincoln in Washington, D.C.*

sym·bol (sĭm′ bəl) *noun* Something that stands for or represents something else: *Each star on the United States flag is a symbol for one of the fifty states.*

T

tend (tĕnd) *verb* To look after; take care of: *Ben tended the garden by pulling weeds and watering the plants.*

ter·ri·fy·ing (tĕr′ ə fī′ ĭng) *adjective* Causing much fear: *The monster in the movie was a terrifying sight.*

the·a·ter (thē′ ə tər) *noun* A building where concerts, plays, and movies are presented: *Ashley would rather listen to a concert in a theater than in a big outdoor park.*

thread (thrĕd) *verb* To pass thread through the eye of a needle or through the hooks and holes on a sewing machine: *Josh threaded a needle to sew the button back on his shirt.*

trek (trĕk) *verb* To make a hard, slow trip: *We were really tired after we trekked up the tall mountain.*

tre·men·dous (trĭ mĕn′ dəs) *adjective* Very great, large, or powerful: *Gloria swung the bat and hit the ball with tremendous force.*

tri·um·phant (trī ŭm′ fənt) *adjective* Successful: *The triumphant runner received a gold medal after the race.*

troop (trōōp) *noun* A group of soldiers: *The brave troops guarded the fort.*

U

un·u·su·al (ŭn yōō′ zhōō əl) *adjective* Not usual, common, or ordinary: *It is unusual for rain to fall in the desert.*

statue

Trek
Trek comes from the Dutch word *trekken*, meaning "to travel." In a South African version of Dutch called *Afrikaans*, the word was used to mean "a journey by ox wagon."

troop

ōō **boo**t / ou **ou**t / ŭ **cu**t / û **fu**r / hw **wh**ich / th **th**in / *th* **th**is / zh vi**si**on / ə **a**go, sil**e**nt, penc**i**l, lem**o**n, circ**u**s

V

victorious

vic·to·ri·ous (vĭk tôr′ ē əs)
adjective Having won by
defeating another person or
group: *The* **victorious** *soccer
team celebrated after the
game.*

vis·i·ble (vĭz′ ə bəl) *adjective*
Able to be seen: *Beth's bright
yellow jacket made her* **visible**
in the crowd.

W

weak·ling (wēk′ lĭng) *noun*
A person or animal without
strength or power: *Compared
to a lion, a house cat is a*
weakling.

wealth (wĕlth) *noun* A great
amount of money or valuable
possessions: *The queen wore
diamonds as a sign of her*
wealth.

wor·ried (wûr′ ēd) *adjective*
Feeling concerned or upset:
Tom was **worried** *that the
quarter would fall out of
his pocket.*

Weakling

Weakling contains
the suffix *-ling,*
which means
"smaller or with
less force." The
suffix *-ling* also
means "a person
or animal that is
young." Another
word that contains
-ling is *duckling.*

ă **r**at / ā **pay** / â c**are** / ä **f**ather / ĕ **p**et / ē b**e** / ĭ **p**it / ī **p**ie / î **fie**rce / ŏ **p**ot /
ō **go** / ô **paw, for** / oi **oil** / o͝o b**oo**k

Acknowledgments

Pronunciation key and definitions © 1998 by Houghton Mifflin Company. Adapted and reprinted by permission from The American Heritage Children's Dictionary.

Main Literature Selections

The Ballad of Mulan. This version of the traditional Chinese story of Mulan was written and illustrated by Song Nan Zhang, and published by Pan Asian Publications (USA) Inc., Union City, California. Copyright © 1998, by Song Nan Zhang. Reprinted by permission of the publisher.

Selection from *Celebrating Chinese New Year,* by Diane Hoyt-Goldsmith, photographs by Lawrence Migdale. Text copyright © 1998 by Diane Hoyt-Goldsmith. Photographs copyright © 1998 by Lawrence Migdale. All rights reserved. Reprinted by permission of Holiday House, Inc.

Excerpt from *Cliff Hanger,* by Jean Craighead George, illustrated by Wendell Minor. Text copyright © 2002 by Julie Productions Inc. Illustrations copyright © 2002 by Wendell Minor. Reprinted by permission of HarperCollins Publishers.

Dancing Rainbows: A Pueblo Boy's Story, by Evelyn Clarke Mott. Copyright © 1996 by Evelyn Clarke Mott. Reprinted by permission of Dutton Children's Books, a division of Penguin Putnam Inc.

Selection from *Dinosaur Bob and His Adventures with the Family Lazardo,* by William Joyce. Copyright © 1988 by William Joyce. Reprinted by permission of HarperCollins Publishers.

Dogzilla, by Dav Pilkey. Copyright © 1993 by Dav Pilkey. Reprinted by permission of Harcourt Inc.

"Fugitives on Four Legs," by Jean Kaplan Teichroew from the June 1999 issue of *National Geographic World.* Copyright © 1999 by the National Geographic Society. Reprinted by permission of National Geographic Society.

The Garden of Abdul Gasazi, by Chris Van Allsburg. Copyright © 1979 by Chris Van Allsburg. Reprinted by permission of Houghton Mifflin Company. All rights reserved.

Excerpt from *Grandma's Records,* by Eric Velasquez. Copyright © 2001 by Eric Velasquez. All rights reserved. Reprinted with permission of Walker & Co.

The Keeping Quilt, by Patricia Polacco. Copyright © 1998 by Patricia Polacco. Reprinted with permission of Simon & Schuster Books for Young Readers, Simon & Schuster Children's Publishing Division. All rights reserved.

The Lost and Found, by Mark Teague, published by Scholastic Press, a division of Scholastic Inc. Copyright © 1998 by Mark Teague. Used by permission of Scholastic Inc.

Selection from *Miss Rumphius,* by Barbara Cooney. Copyright © 1982 by Barbara Cooney. Reprinted by permission of Viking Penguin, an imprint of Penguin Putnam Books for Young Readers, a division of Penguin Putnam Inc. All rights reserved.

The Mysterious Giant of Barletta, by Tomie dePaola. Copyright © 1984 by Tomie dePaola. Reproduced by permission of Harcourt Inc.

Selection from *Radio Rescue,* by Lynne Barasch. Copyright © 2000 by Lynne Barasch. Reprinted by permission of Farrar, Straus and Giroux, LLC.

Raising Dragons, by Jerdine Nolen, illustrated by Elise Primavera. Text copyright © 1998 by Jerdine Nolen. Illustrations copyright © 1998 by Elise Primavera. Reprinted by permission of Harcourt Inc.

Selection from *Sybil Ludington's Midnight Ride,* by Marsha Amstel, published by Carolrhoda Books, Inc., a Division of Lerner Publishing Group. Text copyright © 2000 by Marsha Amstel. Used by permission of the publisher. All rights reserved.

Talented Kids: "Keyed Up" from the December 2001 issue of *National Geographic World.* Copyright © 2001 by the National Geographic Society. Reprinted by permission of the National Geographic Society.

The Talking Cloth, by Rhonda Mitchell. Copyright © 1997 by Rhonda Mitchell. Reprinted by permission of Orchard Books, New York.

Focus Selections

"Andre" from *Bronzeville Boys and Girls,* by Gwendolyn Brooks. Text copyright © 1956 by Gwendolyn Brooks Blakely. Reprinted by permission of HarperCollins Publishers.

"April Rain Song" from *The Collected Poems of Langston Hughes,* by Langston Hughes. Copyright © 1994 by The Estate of Langston Hughes. Reprinted by permission of Alfred A. Knopf, a division of Random House, Inc. and Harold Ober Associates Inc.

"Aunt Fox and the Fried Fish," originally published as "Tia Zorra y los peces," by Rafael Rivero Oramas. Copyright © 1985 Rafael Rivero Oramas. Published in the anthology *El mundo de Tío Conejo.* Copyright © 1985 by Ediciones Ekaré. Reprinted by permission of Ediciones Ekaré.

"The Bat" from *Beast Feast,* by Douglas Florian. Copyright © 1994 by Douglas Florian. Reprinted with permission of Harcourt, Inc.

"Books/Los Libros" from *Angels Ride Bikes and Other Fall Poems,* by Francisco X. Alarcón. Poem copyright © 1999 by Francisco X. Alarcón. Reprinted with the permission of the publisher, Children's Book Press, San Francisco, CA.

"Cloud Dragons," a poem from the book *Confetti: Poems for Children,* by Pat Mora. Copyright © 1996 by Pat Mora. Permission arranged with Lee & Low Books Inc., New York, NY 10016.

"Giraffe" from *Doodle Dandies,* by J. Patrick Lewis, first appeared in Ranger Rick magazine, December 1994. Text copyright © 1998 by J. Patrick Lewis. Reprinted with the permission of Atheneum Books for Young Readers, an imprint of Simon & Schuster Children's Publishing Division.

"Hungry Spider" from *Thirty-Three Multicultural Tales to Tell,* by Pleasant L. DeSpain. Copyright © 1993 by Pleasant L. DeSpain. Used by permission of August House Publishers.

"If I Were an Ant," by Hitomi Takeshi, third grade from *Festival in my Heart: Poems by Japanese Children,* translated by Bruno Navasky, published by Harry N. Abrams, Inc. Copyright © 1993 by Harry N. Abrams, Inc. Reprinted by permission of the publisher. All rights reserved.

"Joe" from *Every Time I Climb a Tree,* by David McCord. Copyright © 1952, renewed 1980 by David McCord.

Reprinted by permission of Little, Brown and Company, (Inc.) and the Estate of David T.W. McCord.

"Rabbit Races with Turtle" from *How Rabbit Tricked Otter and Other Cherokee Trickster Stories,* by Gayle Ross. Copyright © 1994 by Gayle Ross. Published by permission of PARABOLA Magazine; WWW.PARABOLA.ORG.

"Show Fish" from *Falling Up,* by Shel Silverstein. Copyright © 1996 by Shel Silverstein. Reprinted by permission of HarperCollins Publishers.

"Sneeze" from *No One Writes a Letter to the Snail,* by Maxine Kumin. Text copyright © 1962 by Maxine W. Kumin. Reprinted by permission of The Anderson Literary Agency, Inc.

"Spaghetti! Spaghetti!" from *Rainy, Rainy Saturday,* by Jack Prelutsky. Text copyright © 1980 by Jack Prelutsky. Reprinted by permission of HarperCollins Publishers.

Links and Theme Openers

"Chinese The Write Way," text by Susan Wills, illustrated by YongSheng Xuan, from *SPIDER the Magazine for Children,* August 1996 issue, Vol. 3, No. 8. Text copyright © 1996 by Susan Wills. Illustrations copyright © 1996 by YongSheng Xuan. Cover copyright © 1996 by Carus Publishing Company. Reprinted by permission of the author and illustrator. Cover reprinted by permission of SPIDER Magazine.

"Eyes on Rome" from the July 1995 issue of *National Geographic World.* Copyright © 1995 by National Geographic Society. Reprinted by permission of the National Geographic Society.

"Go with the Flow" from the May 1997 issue of *3 2 1 Contact* magazine. Copyright © 1997 by Children's Television Workshop. Reprinted by arrangement with the publisher. All rights reserved.

"A Healthy Recipe from Ghana," originally published as "Homemade Peanut Butter" is reprinted from *The Kids' Multicultural Cookbook.* Copyright © 1995 by Williamson Publishing.

"The House I Live In," words and music by Lewis Allan and Earl Robinson. Copyright © 1942 (Renewed) Chappell & Co., Inc. All Rights Reserved. Used by permission of Warner Bros. Publications U.S. Inc., Miami, FL 33014.

"I Lost the Work I Found" from *The Goof Who Invented Homework and Other School Poems,* by Kalli Dakos, illustrated by Denise Brunkus. Text copyright © 1996 by Kalli Dakos. Reprinted by permission of Dial Books for Young Readers, a division of Penguin Putnam Inc.

"Lost," by Bruce Lansky. Copyright © 1997 by Bruce Lansky. Reprinted by permission of Meadowbrook Press.

"Nesting Dolls," by Marie Kingdon from *Hopscotch for Girls,* Vol. 10, No. 2, August/ September 1998. Copyright © 1998 by Marie Kingdon. Reprinted by permission of the publisher.

"Rain and Rainbows," originally published as "Rain Catcher" and "Rain of Color" from *The Science Book of Weather,* by Neil Ardley. Copyright © 1992 by Neil Ardley. Copyright © 1992 by Dorling Kindersley, Ltd. London. Reprinted by permission of Harcourt, Inc.

"Read. . . Think. . . Dream," by J. Patrick Lewis. Copyright © 1992 by J. Patrick Lewis. Reprinted by permission of the author.

"Real-Life Dragons," originally published as "Do You Believe in Dragons?" by Robert Gray. Reprinted from the October 1993 issue of *Ranger Rick* magazine with the permission of the publisher, the National Wildlife Federation. Copyright © 1993 by the National Wildlife Federation.

"September Yearning" from *Gingerbread Days,* by Joyce Carol Thomas, illustrations by Floyd Cooper. Text copyright © 1995 by Joyce Carol Thomas. Illustrations copyright © 1995 by Floyd Cooper. Used by permission of HarperCollins Publishers. All rights reserved.

Talented Kids: "Music Maestro" from the November 1999 issue of *National Geographic World.* Copyright © 1999 by the National Geographic Society. Reprinted by permission of the National Geographic Society.

Talented Kids: "Sounds Great!" from the November 1998 issue of *National Geographic World.* Copyright © 1998 by the National Geographic Society. Reprinted by permission of the National Geographic Society.

Talented Kids: "Young Mariachi Music Makers," by Ann Jordan from *APPLESEEDS'* March 2000 issue: Fiesta!. Copyright © 2000 by Cobblestone Publishing, 30 Grove Street, Suite C, Peterborough, NH 03458. All rights reserved. Reproduced by permission of Cobblestone Publishing Company.

"These Kids Rock" was originally published as "Rock Climbing Kids," by Deborah Churchman in the November 2000 issue of *Ranger Rick* magazine. Copyright © 2000 by the National Wildlife Federation. Reprinted with the permission of the publisher, the National Wildlife Federation.

Additional Acknowledgments

Special thanks to the following teachers whose students' compositions appear as Student Writing Models: Cindy Cheatwood, Florida; Diana Davis, North Carolina; Kathy Driscoll, Massachusetts; Linda Evers, Florida; Heidi Harrison, Michigan; Eileen Hoffman, Massachusetts; Bonnie Lewison, Florida; Kanetha McCord, Michigan.

Credits

Photography

1 (t) © David Mendelsohn/Masterfile. (m) Tomi/PhotoLink/Photodisc Green/Getty Images. (b) Jody Dole/The Image Bank/Getty Images. **3** © David Mendelsohn/Masterfile. **6** Tomi/PhotoLink/Photodisc Green/Getty Images. **9** Jody Dole/The Image Bank/Getty Images. **10-11** (bkgd) © Ariel Skelley/CORBIS. **11** (m) © David Mendelsohn/Masterfile. **12** Courtesy of Mark Teague. **16-17** (bkgd) © Royalty-Free/CORBIS. **16** © Dorling Kindersley. **17** (tl) © Peter Mathis/STONE/ Getty Images. (tr) © Dorling Kindersley. (b) © Steve Starr/IndexStock Imagery. **18** (t) Courtesy Jean Craighead George. (b) Courtesy Wendell Minor. Photo: Charlie Craighead copyright 2001. **18** (frames) © PhotoDisc/Getty Images. **18-19** (bkgd) © Ken Redding/CORBIS. **46-49** Jackson Smith Photography. **52** (l) © Royal Ontario Museum/CORBIS. (br) © Seattle Art Museum/ CORBIS. **53** (r)© Royal Ontario Museum/ CORBIS. (b) © Keren Su/CORBIS. **54** Courtesy, Song Nan Zhang. **54-5** (bkgd) © Steve Vidler/ SuperStock. **92** Michael Greenlar/ Mercury Pictures. **122-3** (bkgd) © James P. Blair/National Geographic/Getty Images. **122** (b) © David Mendelsohn/ Masterfile. **160-1** (bkgd) © Jonathan Blair/Corbis. **160** Lawrence Migdale. **184-5** Private Collection of Karen A. Fecko. **186** © Joseph Sohm; ChromoSohm Inc./CORBIS. **188** © PhotoDisc/ Getty Images. **189** (tl) © Royalty-Free/CORBIS. (r) HMCo film archive. (b) ©Angelo

Cavalli/SuperStock. **190-1** © W. Cody/Corbis. **190**
Michael Tamborino/ Mercury Pictures. **210-13** (bkgd) ©
Geoff Brightling/ Taxi/Getty Images. **210** (inset)) Walter
P. Calahan. **211** (inset) Steven M. Herppich/The
Cincinnati Enquirer. **212** (inset) VSA Arts Panasonic
Young Soloists Program. Photo: Courtesy Victor and
Belina Mendoza. **213** (inset) Ann Jordan. **214** ©
Lawrence Migdale/Mira. **215** (t) © Robert Frerck/
Odyssey/Chicago. (b) © Margaret Courtney-
Clark/CORBIS. **216** Kathie Lentz. **216-7** (bkgd) © Owen
Franken/ Corbis. **234** (banner) © PhotoDisc/Getty
Images. (l) © John Running. **235** (all) © Stephen Trimble.
236-7 (bkgd) © Discovery Comm/Panoramic Images. **236**
Courtesy, Evelyn Clarke Mott. **237–55** © Evelyn Clarke
Mott. **258** © PhotoDisc/Getty Images. **260-1** (bkgd) ©
Charles Gold/CORBIS. **260** (b) Tomi/PhotoLink/
Photodisc Green/Getty Images. **274–276** Lawrence
Migdale. **302-3** (bkgd) (ship) © Austin Brown/Stone/
Getty Images. (book) (clouds) (wave) © PhotoDisc/Getty
Images. **303** (m) Jody Dole/The Image Bank/Getty
Images. **304** Courtesy of Jerdine Nolan. **308** Corbis/Paul
Kaye; Cordaiy Photo Library Ltd. **309** (t) Cinema
Memories. (b) Movie Still Archives. **310** (bkgd) © David
Zimmerman/Corbis. **329** Courtesy, Grolier Inc./Orchard
Books. **332** (t) Corbis/Roger Ressmeyer. **336** (banner) ©
PhotoDisc/Getty Images. (b) © F. Stella/Marka. **337** (t) ©
F. Stella/Marka. (b) © Giuliano Colliva/The Image
Bank/Getty Images. **338** © Suki Coughlin. **338-9** (bkgd)
Joe Cornish/Stone/Getty Images. **358-61** (all) Richard
Nowitz/NGS Image Collection. **362** (t) © Curt Maas/
Stone/Getty Images. (b) Larry Lefever/Grant Heilman
Photography Inc. **363** (tl) (bl) Larry Lefever/Grant
Heilman Photography Inc. **364-5** (bkgd) William A. Bake/
The Image Bank/Getty Images. **364** (t) Dennis Crews/
Mercury Pictures. (b) Barry Korbman/Mercury Pictures.
390 © Hans & Judy Beste/Lochman Transparencies. **391**
Masahiro Iijima/Nature Production. **392** (b) © Jean-Paul
Ferrero/Auscape. **392-3** (t) Stephen Dalton/Animals
Animals. **394** © Robin Shields/Mercury Pictures. **395** (t)
Leo de Wys Inc./W. Hille. (b) © Robin Shields/ Mercury
Pictures. **396** Scott Goodwin Photography. **396-7** (bkgd)
© Michael Boys/ Corbis. **416-17** Scott Goodwin
Photography. **417** (cl) sketch for *Jumanji* © Chris Van
Allsburg. Courtesy of The Kerlan Collection, University of
Minnesota. **419** Courtesy, Chris Van Allsburg. **420-1**
(bkgd) © Per-Eric Berglund/The Image Bank/Getty
Images. **420** (b) Jody Dole/The Image Bank/Getty Images.
422–23 Patrick Ward/National Geographic Society **441**
©Philadelphia Museum of Art/CORBIS. **442** © Morton
Beebe, S.F./CORBIS. **443** (t) © Mark Gibson/CORBIS.
(b) © Peter Turnley/CORBIS. **444** (t) © Randy
Faris/CORBIS. (b) © Richard Hamilton Smith/CORBIS.
445 (t) © Lynda Richardson/CORBIS. (c) (b) © Kelly-
Mooney Photography/CORBIS. **446** © TempSport/
CORBIS.

Assignment Photography
418 (tl) © HMCo./Karen Ahola. **85** (r), **90-91, 116,
158** (b), **159, 232-33, 259, 363** (r), **389** (r), **415** (l) ©
HMCo./Joel Benjamin. **332-33** (b) © HMCo./Kim
Holcombe. **181** (ml, mr), **231** (ml, mr), **257** (ml, mr) ©
HMCo./Jack Holtel. **137,279,439** © HMCo./Michael
Indresano Photography.

Illustration
12–15 Mark Teague. **118-19** Jean Hirashima. **121** Floyd
Cooper. **87-88** Lily Toy Hong. **131–4** Neal Armstrong.
145 Susan Swan. **146** Elizabeth Sayles. **147** Liz Callen.
148 Susan Swan. **149** Shel Silverstein. **154–5** Patricia
Polacco. **180** (bl) **256** (b) Mercedes McDonald. **258-59**
Michael Sloan. **280-81** Mary Grandpré. **282-87, 300** (t)
Daniel Moreton. **288-93, 300** (bl) copyright © 2001 by
Murv Jacob. **294-99, 300** (br) Richard Bernal. **415, 417,
418** Chris Van Allsburg.